MARC

THE
CONTAGIOUS
CATHOLIC

The Art of Practical Evangelization

ASCENSION

West Chester, Pennsylvania

Ascension
Post Office Box 1990
West Chester, PA 19380
1-800-376-0520
ascensionpress.com

Cover design by Rosemary Strohm

Printed in the United States of America
20 21 22 23 24 5 4 3 2 1
ISBN 978-1-950784-24-0

CONTENTS

FOREWORD

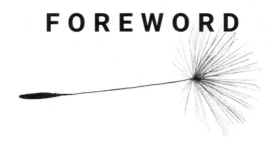

This generation of Catholics is responsible for this generation of people. We live in a Church that seems to have forgotten her evangelical imperative (at least in the first world). There are literally billions of people who live in dire poverty, waiting to be enriched by the love and care of dedicated missionary disciples. Whether these people lack food, clean water, medicine, or safety, or they are trapped in slavery, they need to be rescued. To rescue people is the mission of the Church. And the greatest form of poverty—the gateway to all other forms of poverty—is not knowing the one true God, not knowing his merciful work of salvation, offered in the life, death, and resurrection of Jesus Christ, and not living in covenantal love with him. Caring for people, in the here and now, is critically important, and bringing eternal life to their immortal souls is absolutely essential. " 'We wish to confirm once more that the task of evangelizing all people constitutes the essential mission of the Church.' ... Evangelizing is in fact the grace and vocation proper to the Church, her deepest identity. She exists in order to evangelize" (Paul VI, *Evangelii Nuntiandi*, 14).

Over the past twenty years, there has been a wonderful reawakening of a sense of the importance of evangelization. When FOCUS (Fellowship of Catholic University Students) was launched in 1998, I frequently heard comments like, "Are you sure evangelization is something Catholics do?" Today, thanks to the work of many—and particularly St. John Paul II, Pope Benedict XVI, and Pope Francis— engaged Catholics have a desire to evangelize. But they may not know how to do so. That is where *The Contagious Catholic* comes in: Marcel LeJeune has been at the tip of the spear in the New Evangelization for decades. His practical insights, based upon faithfulness to Church teaching and drawn from fruitful work with tens of thousands, make him an ideal instructor.

The story is often told of an elementary school teacher who was teaching her class. At one point, she realized that the students were not tracking with what she was trying to say. Looking at the board in the front of the class, where there were two words written, the teacher realized that maybe the students did not know what they meant. So she asked, "Can anyone tell me the difference between 'ignorance' and 'apathy'?" There was silence. Turning to the star student, MariAnna, the teacher tried again. "MariAnna, can you tell us the difference between 'ignorance' and 'apathy'?" MariAnna paused for a moment and then responded, "I don't know, and I don't care." And there is the difference between ignorance and apathy.

Both questions that this difference provokes are important: "Why should I care?" will lift the apathetic, and "How do I do this?" will guide the ignorant. The world yearns to be evangelized so that they will care. Disciples need to be taught how to be missionary disciples so that they can evangelize. Marcel LeJeune offers the best "how-to" that I have seen. After building the case from Church teaching that we ought to be an evangelizing people, he gets practical. He offers concrete examples and specific actions so that we can begin to evangelize the people in our lives.

St. Augustine, in his masterful work *The City of God*, offers a worldview of humanity divided into two "cities." The first is the City of God and is populated by those who love God so much that they would be willing to deny even themselves. The second is the City of Man and is filled with those who love themselves so much that they would be willing to deny even God. St. Augustine saw this as the essential story of human history, the great battle that extends across all people and all millennia. Those who live and die in the City of Man will spend eternity separated from God. Those who live and die in the City of God will spend eternity with God. In our distracted lives, we often forget this basic truth that St. John Henry Newman reminded us of: Everyone who ever lived, still does, somewhere.

From this perspective, the only thing that can ultimately matter is coming to live in the City of God. No amount of earthly success, fame, or fortune will offset an eternity separated from God. There are only two ways for Jesus' followers to grow the City of God: procreation and evangelization. We must always work to alleviate the suffering of others, but we must be willing to suffer misfortune and inconvenience to live in the City of God and to help others do so as well through evangelization. The world is increasingly filled with distractions, but only one thing truly matters: living in the City of God. And to live in the City of God, Jesus told us to "seek first his kingdom and his righteousness, and all these things shall be yours as well" (Matthew 6:33). When we seek first his kingdom—when we allow Marcel LeJeune's insights to enrich our evangelization efforts—we will be able to do the work of Martha in Mary's spirit (Luke 10:38-42) and alleviate poverty in all its forms.

I hope that you will enjoy *The Contagious Catholic* as much as I did. Even more, I hope that you will embrace the principles in the book to change the way you live so that you will become a missionary disciple maker. Don't stop there—share the book with others and invite them to become contagious Catholics, too!

Curtis A. Martin
FOCUS founder
October 1, 2019
Feast of St. Thérèse of the Child Jesus,
Patroness of the Missions

INTRODUCTION

I contracted chicken pox as a child like many others before me. From my perspective as a kid, it was an awful situation. Not only did I feel terrible, but I couldn't even be around those who had not had the virus. I was contagious and did not want others to get sick, so I was quarantined from most of my friends and family.

In today's Catholic culture, we often act like we have quarantined our faith from others. Yet we don't have a virus—we are faithful Catholics who have Jesus in our lives. A Catholic life without evangelization means living as if we fear others might end up having Jesus in their lives too. Yet this is the opposite of how we ought to live. We ought to be contagious, not quarantined. We ought to spread the love of Jesus we have in our lives. We need to evangelize.

God loves us so much, we ought to fear that any of his creatures could die and not go to heaven. This fear ought to drive us out into the streets. But fear isn't enough. Love is.

Think of these two truths: (1) We are called to love others. (2) The most loving thing we could do for another person is to help him or her grow closer to God, who is love itself.

If these are both true, then we cannot say we love others and fail to evangelize!

A life without evangelization is quarantined, safe, and fruitless. This is how I lived for many years. When I was finally convinced that I needed to start sharing my faith, though, I failed miserably. In fact, I probably drove away more people than I helped. I thought winning an argument, being upset when someone said something I found offensive, or convincing someone to admit that I was right was in fact "evangelization." It wasn't. It was merely my sins, wounds, and fears coming to the surface.

Through it all, God worked on my heart. I stopped talking quite so much and started to listen. I learned to respond appropriately. Instead of launching into a monologue about apologetics every time, I entered into dialogue and found out when apologetics were truly needed. I am still working on my pride and my fears, because we all struggle with sin, yet I am more fruitful than ever before. This is not because I am a radically different person but because I am more radically open to letting God work through me. I truly believe he does work through his people. God wants to work through you in a powerful way!

I worked fifteen years in campus ministry. For most of that time, I ran the day-to-day operations of one of the largest Catholic campus ministries in the world. No matter what else I did at work, I never stopped meeting in small groups and meeting one-on-one with students. I knew that the greatest thing we could offer others was not just a program, event, or class but rather a relationship with a mature Catholic who was a missionary disciple. Through working with students, I learned many lessons. My experience in ministry has led me to write about evangelization on my blog and to share many lessons with you throughout this book.

The first thing you ought to know is this—the best way to be a better evangelist is to go out and try to evangelize, fail, learn how to do it better, and then do it again. The students I worked with on campus taught me more about what not to do, through those fifteen years, than any book ever could. The world needs you to do this. Someone out there right now needs you to do this.

Abby Johnson needed me to do this. You may have heard of Abby because she is a pro-life speaker who was a former Planned Parenthood clinic director. I was blessed to have the opportunity to help Abby and her husband, Doug, explore the Catholic Faith. Like most people who have been wrestling with faith, Abby and Doug had some rough spots, just as I did. They also had a lot of very hard questions about difficult subjects. We went through them all. Sometimes they challenged me. Sometimes I challenged them. We prayed together, we got to know one another, and we walked toward Jesus together. Ultimately, they both had conversions, became Catholic, and are now missionary disciples.

The next step is for you and me to become more fruitful disciples of Jesus who are better evangelists. We do this for our own souls, the souls of others, the growth of the Church, and the glory of God. That is what being a Catholic is all about.

CHAPTER 1

FOLLOWING JESUS

It was one of the most embarrassing moments of my college years. I asked a beautiful young woman (who is now my wife) on a date, and after we finished our meal, the check came, as always. That's when I realized I had forgotten my wallet at home! I like to say that I no longer have awkward moments, but having to ask my date to pay for our meal was definitely one. It was humbling to realize I had received something I didn't have the ability to pay for.

This is somewhat like the gift of heaven. We all want to end up in heaven, but none of us have the ability to pay for our own salvation with our own merit. Only Jesus has the ability to pay the price to open the gates of heaven for us. Jesus, God made man, laid down his life for sinners—you and me. Why would God do this?

It is because you and I matter to God. God loves us. He created us out of a sheer act of love. We are made to live in this love, receive it, offer it back to him, and give it to others. He sees in us an unending dignity and worth. He cares for us. He longs for relationship with us. In fact, God's greatest desire is to have an everlasting relationship with us!

Most of us will not doubt these truths, at least not on the surface. In fact, you may have heard "God loves you" thousands of times, but do you know how much value God sees in you?

To illustrate, ask yourself what you would do if you dropped your wedding ring—would you pick it up? Of course you would because it is valuable to you. Now, what about a penny? It probably depends on the situation because a penny is not as valuable.

To God, you are not a penny. You are not even a wedding ring. You are much more valuable to God than any object. In fact, he is working hard, right now, to get you to heaven. He is close to you. He is loving you, right where you are. He has given you grace and will continue to do so.

The Catholic Church also has a role in this relationship between humans and God. The Church is meant to be a channel of this powerful grace to its members so they can then be channels of grace to others. The Church (you and I) "exists in order to evangelize, that is to say, in order to preach and teach, to be the channel of the gift of grace, to reconcile sinners with God, and to perpetuate Christ's sacrifice in the Mass, which is the memorial of His death and glorious resurrection."[1]

The Church exists to make disciples of the world—to evangelize. The word *evangelization* comes from the Greek *euangelion*, which means "good news." To bring good news is our vocation as disciples. And not just any good news, but *the* Good News, the resurrected Jesus. The one who conquers death and sin. We, his followers, are made to be missionaries, and our mission field is all of humanity.

From here we could complain about the decline of the Church in the West and how the Catholic Church in the United States is losing more than six people for every one person who converts to Catholicism.[2] But that is not what this book is about. Rather, this book is about helping Catholics who want to evangelize more effectively in the real world, which means helping others become better missionary disciples. This starts by caring about what God cares about so we can have the same desires God has.

Do we really and truly care about what God cares about? If not, then the issue lies within our own hearts, and this book will do no good. We can learn all the great techniques the Church can teach about evangelization, but if we do not love and care about what God loves and cares about, we are not going to evangelize. No amount of education or strategy can cover up for apathy. Now, I really hate to make assumptions, but if you read on from this point, I'm going to make one. I am assuming you do care about what God cares about, at some level. In other words, you love people.

Strategy and technique mean nothing if we do not love the person in front of us. The strategy that matters most is to love others and find joy in Jesus.

So the issue we need to address lies in *how* we love others. The mission of Jesus while he was on earth was to save the world from sin and death so that salvation in heaven is possible. This is now the Church's mission. This is our mission. This is *your* mission. So how are you doing? Are you fruitful? Are others experiencing conversion due to your life, words, and work? Do you try to evangelize in some way?

Jesus never asked his followers to do anything he did not do. We see it repeated in the Gospels again and again—

Jesus went to others to bring the message of salvation to them. He did not wait for them to come to him. We, too, are called to go evangelize the world if we are Jesus' followers. There is no backup plan of evangelization—*we* are the means by which Jesus' plan will be implemented in our day and age.

So, if we are disciples of Jesus, we ought to care for what he cares for. We need to do what he calls us to do. We need to love as God loves. We need to love others enough to make them aware of Jesus' love for them. Notice that this is not bringing God to them—he is already present in some way to them. Our goal is to make his presence known.

This task sometimes seems impossible. Jesus came and died. He rose from the dead, ascended to heaven, sent the Holy Spirit, and commissioned the Church to continue what he started. But none of us is God. Jesus is God, and he still didn't finish the job, so how are we supposed to do it? Well, we sometimes overthink, overanalyze, and overtrain for it— so much so that we just do not actually do it very much.

Recently, my wife and I went on a wonderful vacation to New Orleans with some friends. When we returned home, our family and friends asked us about the vacation. I was excited to tell them about our experiences—what we did, the food we ate, how much we enjoyed it, and more. It was a great story to tell. But imagine if I refused to tell my family and friends about my vacation until I had trained and equipped myself to talk about it. The story certainly would not have been told with the same vigor or detail because that wears off. In fact, I may not have told any stories at all if I first had to watch a video training, read a book, or attend a conference on how to tell people about New Orleans. We need to treat evangelization in the same way. While educating, training, and equipping others is good (and is the reason for this book), we will never be the evangelists Jesus wants us to be until we start to live a life where the grace of God pours out of us naturally.

There are several things that might hold us back. In our honest moments, we can admit that most of us are frightened of evangelization. Maybe we do not have the skills of those we consider great evangelists. Our personalities are not suited to the task. We are busy. We worry about the reactions of others. We don't know what we are doing. We have a million excuses—at least I know I do. I certainly am not the perfect evangelist. I can be grumpy, sarcastic, and prideful. I like to fix more than listen. Yet I have this deep desire to see salvation come to the world. So I do imperfect evangelization anyway, and God has used my meager offering to change hearts. As Paul said, "For the sake of Christ, then, I am content with weaknesses, insults, hardships, persecutions, and calamities; for when I am weak, then I am strong" (2 Corinthians 12:10).

Only disciples of Jesus make other disciples of Jesus. That means the point of our Christian existence is to multiply ourselves as best we can before we leave this earth and join God in heaven forever. But first we must address the elephant in the room: Most Catholics are not very good at evangelization for one reason or another. I believe the two biggest reasons are that (1) we are not using Jesus' strategy (plan of action), and (2) we do not love others enough. This book will focus primarily on the first reason. But the second is vitally important, too.

DISCIPLESHIP –
DOING WHAT THE MASTER DID

Imagine you are allowed to participate in the pregame preparation of your favorite college basketball team before it plays in the national championship game. You are in the locker room. The coach is about to lay out the strategy for how to beat the other team, which is faster, bigger, stronger, and more talented. The coach says, "We are going to get out there and beat the other team. We are going to win the game by scoring more points than our opponent. Go!"

That team will most likely lose. Why? Because the coach did not give an actual strategy for how to win, just a goal to achieve. The real question left unanswered is *how* to win the game. What strategy will be used?

This is how many Catholics operate, both individually and in parishes, apostolates, and dioceses. We run programs, we invite folks to Mass, we have classes, we go to conferences and retreats. These are good things. But making disciples is so much more. We need a strategy.

We need to get back to the basics of *what, why, where,* and *how.*

- *Mission* tells us *what* we are doing. The mission of the Catholic Church is to "go ... and make disciples of all nations" (Matthew 28:19).

- *Values* tell us *why* we do what we do. The values of the Catholic Church are faithfulness to God for the good of humanity.

- *Vision* tells us *where* we are going—where God wants us to go. The vision of the Church is that God wants us all to be holy saints in heaven.

- *Strategy* tells us *how* we will achieve the vision. This is the tough one. Strategy asks how Jesus wants us to operate in order to fulfill his commands to evangelize.

Strategy is what is haunting most Catholics. We have great mission, values, and vision for the Church, which were given to us by Jesus when he said, "All authority in heaven and on earth has been given to me. Go therefore and make disciples of all nations, baptizing them in the name of the Father and of the Son and of the Holy Spirit, teaching them to observe all that I have commanded you; and behold, I am with you always, to the close of the age" (Matthew 28:18-20). We know what we ought to achieve, why it is important, and where we are headed. The big question is: *How* do we achieve these things? This is where the rubber meets the road.

Hundreds of books from business gurus, pastors, and other leaders could fill up a library on mission statements, visionary leadership, and strategic thinking. But, as Catholics, we need to mine the depths of wisdom already passed down to us and then apply that wisdom to twenty-first-century Western culture.

We do not need a new *what*, *why*, *where*, or even a new *how*. We just need to believe that Jesus truly has answers to his Church's present needs and that he calls us to be faithful to the mission he gave us.

Furthermore, a good strategy for evangelization is not something accomplished by merely laying out a well-planned idea that is executed and then brings others to faith. That would make it merely a human work. Rather, having an evangelization strategy is a cooperation with the work of the Holy Spirit, who impels us to go out and evangelize but who does the hard work of moving another person's heart to conversion. (And the person cooperates by giving consent.) It is also built upon the teaching and methodology of Jesus, who revealed how he wants us to evangelize by the way he lived his life and the words he said. This means the pressure is off us.

God merely wants to work through us, but in order to do that, we have to give him permission. Thus, making a gift of our will by consenting to his grace over and over again is the way we participate in the redemption of the world. God wants to use us as his instruments, but we have to allow God to get our own sin, woundedness, weakness, and pride out of the way. We have to be fully human, which means we need to follow the lead of Jesus. As Vatican II says, "The truth is that only in the mystery of the incarnate Word does the mystery of man take on light."[3] If we want to know who we are meant to be, then we need to get to know Jesus.

WHO WE TRULY ARE

As we dive deep into our true identity as baptized sons and daughters of God, we are able to be more authentically the people God has made us to be—holy saints who can change the world. More our true selves. More authentically human. This authenticity is a hallmark of Jesus and all great evangelists. Jesus was not afraid to show his true self to others if they were willing to receive him. He cried, got angry, celebrated, challenged others, and lived with others through intimate and authentic relationships.

Our job then is to mine the depths of the life of Jesus and his most fruitful followers—the great saints and evangelists—in order to understand what we can about his strategy for evangelization. We need to know what they knew in order better to see the world through the eyes of Jesus so we can reach the world with his grace.

This new way of seeing the world means we have to be willing to risk loss. Jesus risked everything, and his love for us cost him his life. Most of us will not have to lose our lives, but we will suffer the loss of our own way of doing things. We may lose our own dreams for our lives. We may lose relationships when others reject us. There is always a risk in loving others. But in return we gain everything. We gain an eternity of perpetual bliss. We gain true fulfillment. In order to do this, we need to allow ourselves to be challenged continually and then entrust our hearts more fully to Jesus. We need a Catholic worldview—we need to understand the world as the Church does and love it with the heart of Jesus.

This new way of seeing and loving the world changes everything because the way we view the world reflects our philosophy of life and affects our way of thinking about the world. It's a big deal.

Our "worldview glasses" affect how we look at the world and what we see, but most of us don't know we're wearing them. Others may not know their own view, but it's important for us as Catholic evangelists to do our best to understand what their worldview is. When we know where others are coming from, we have a better chance to help them.

If we see the world as God sees the world, then how can we not share the Good News and seek conversion of hearts? If heaven and hell are real, then how can we not seek salvation for others? Those who do not follow Jesus are like the prodigal son, "lost" and "dead" (Luke 15:32). His desire is for them to be found and to be resurrected to a new life.

Ultimately, having good strategy, processes, systems, and programs means nothing if we are not helping transform people because we love them. God's goal is to transform people, and only transformed people are able to help renew the Church. Only someone who consents to transformation is a disciple. As St. John Paul II said,

> It is true that being a Christian means saying "yes" to Jesus Christ, but let us remember that this "yes" has two levels: It consists in surrendering to the word of God and relying on it, but it also means, at a later stage, endeavoring to know better—and better the profound meaning of this word.[4]

BE INTERESTED IN PEOPLE

Jesus found people interesting. He loved to meet them, talk to them, be with them. He asked a lot of questions. He told stories. He listened to their questions and sought out the downtrodden and outcast. If we are following his lead, then we should find people interesting, too. Everyone has stories. Everyone is made in God's image. Everyone has inherent dignity. Everyone desires others to be interested in him or her. Everyone is meant to have a life of purpose. We can learn from others. As Catholics, we ought to be deeply interested in other human beings because we understand just how much God loves the person in front of us.

This is not merely a clever strategy. Rather, it is acting in accord with reality. We are made for one another. We are made to be in relationship with each other. When we bring authentic relationships into the world, it becomes a place of encounter. Then we can win the right to evangelize others. Love demands that we ultimately get to explicit evangelization, but we need not jump right into the deep end. Moving too fast creates barriers to effective evangelization. On the other hand, we should also not avoid or delay too long out of fear.

What is better for any human than to come into a relationship with Jesus, a relationship that leads to salvation? Nothing. That is why Catholics who love others are evangelists.

Evangelization is not something we check off a list. It is not just meeting once a week at church to do a book study. It is not just bringing someone to a conference once in a while. Rather, we want to be real friends to others and intimately share in one another's lives. That means we care for those around us. We want to know their hearts. Once this happens, others will want to know our hearts, as well. What they should find there is the treasure they have always looked for: Jesus.

This kind of friendship is reflected in what happens in the first chapter of the Gospel of John. St. Andrew, who is a disciple of John the Baptist, begins to follow Jesus, and Jesus turns and asks Andrew what he wants. Andrew responds by asking Jesus where he is staying. Jesus says, "Come and see" (John 1:39). From there, a friendship begins. This friendship spills over with love and joy, and Andrew cannot wait to tell his brother, Simon (St. Peter), that he has found the Messiah. Peter has someone fish for him before he ever goes fishing for men.

This is what Christian life and evangelization should look like. Not a project or program but a lifestyle born out of the joy of friendship with Jesus. Think of your best friend when you were a child. That person probably brought you great joy. If you made a new friend who did not know your best friend, you probably could not wait to introduce the two of them. This is because they both brought joy to your life. You were interested in them and they in you. You loved both of them, and you wanted them to experience the joy and friendship you had with each of them.

This is what evangelization is: joyfully introducing a friend to our best friend, Jesus. It is not merely sharing rules, doctrines, pious practices, or prayers, even though those are all good things. Since we can't give what we don't have, it all starts from our own relationship with Jesus and then flows out from there.

METHODOLOGY AND THEOLOGY

Our methodology should reflect our theology because we will live as we truly believe. An examination of what we believe about God and the Catholic Church can help us become better evangelists. For instance, we believe "with God all things are possible" (Matthew 19:26). Therefore, we should not limit God's grace in our lives. Believe he is powerful enough to work through us.

Consider the incarnation of Jesus. He came in flesh so that he could enter into relationship with others. He did not see relationships with people as an obstacle to his mission. Quite the opposite—we are the object of his mission!

The work of evangelization is not about having a formula, doing the right event, running a program, reading a book (including this one), or watching a video series. These are all good things, but when they replace the personal relationship where a Christian disciple walks with others, we get the results we have now. And the culture we have now is a post-Christian culture that is disinterested in the message of Jesus because people think all we want to do is make them into a project, not love them.

Twentieth-century strategies for evangelization stopped working generations ago. So why think they will work for a twenty-first-century culture and people? They won't. Rather, we need to bring the strategy of Jesus into the culture for the people of today.

More and more, the culture rejects what the Catholic Church teaches. In fact, Catholic teaching is considered hateful and mean to many. As Catholics, we have to be willing to take the arrows of criticism. We must not just defend the truth but live the truth. We have to be willing to show that doctrine is not just about having the right answer but about having a life that has been transformed and therefore lives for something greater than self.

Even the ideas of hell and salvation through Jesus are widely considered judgmental and distasteful. Yet we believe these truths. How do we earn the right to make them known to others? The answer is not just to try to bring a friend to Mass or RCIA. That will not work anymore because the vast majority are not interested in going to church. Most non-Catholics have no interest in even considering Catholicism. Until we return to relational evangelization, the Church will continue to have little impact in transforming people's lives in twenty-first-century US culture.

A problem for many Catholics is the idea of "professionalized" evangelization. Many believe it is the job of clergy and religious (and sometimes lay professionals who work in ministry) to evangelize others. Yet the truth is that all baptized and confirmed Catholics are called to the mission field.

Parish and diocesan staff will tell you that the moment most of them stepped into their jobs, they did not have enough time to take care of their existing duties. This often means that they do not have time to do the work of evangelization. Furthermore, most people who work in Catholic institutions have little or no contact with folks who are far away from the Church. To evangelize, we must have contact with others. If we are to reach the world, then, the average Catholic needs to become an evangelist.

Paul told Timothy, who was a bishop, to "do the work of an evangelist, fulfil your ministry" (2 Timothy 4:5). So we should expect our pastors to evangelize, but we cannot wait for them to do it before we do it. Our own obedience to the call to evangelize should never depend on the faithfulness of another.

Jesus is ultimately the model of all of our evangelization because he is the greatest evangelist. He can hold all things in perfect balance. He is loving but challenges others. He preaches difficult truths but is kind in doing so. He can rebuke hypocritical leaders but comfort those who are outcasts. He does all these things while showing us how we ought to evangelize.

Theology informs methodology.

THE COST OF STAYING COMFORTABLE

What would have happened if the apostles had stayed in the upper room after Pentecost? We would probably not be disciples of Jesus today if they had. They needed to go into the world in order to evangelize. Too often we have lost this imperative of our faith—to go out.

Many of us are ready, willing, and able to invest thousands of dollars, thousands of hours of labor, and our own time and effort into programs at our parish, but we never intentionally invest in our neighbors and coworkers who do not go to church and do not know Jesus. We have forgotten how to "go," preferring to stay in the safe bubble of our parish. Instead, the parish should be a home base for outreach, ministry, and evangelization.

The holy boldness of the early Christians has been replaced by merely fulfilling our duty and going to Mass. Speaking boldly about Jesus is scary. We talk ourselves out of doing the scary and difficult work of going out to the world and settle for staying busy at church.

We think of really successful Catholics today as those who go to Mass every Sunday, participate in the sacraments, and pray and tithe. We need to be honest about what keeps us from evangelizing. We need to stop hiding from our fears and being afraid of how others perceive us. We don't need cool. We need courage.

In Luke 12:11-12, Jesus says, "When they bring you before the synagogues and the rulers and the authorities, do not be anxious about how or what you are to answer or what you are to say; for the Holy Spirit will teach you in that very hour what you ought to say."

If we want intimacy with the Holy Spirit, then we must do things that are frightening. In the midst of our faithfulness, which conquers our fears, we will find the Holy Spirit willing to help us. If we are baptized and confirmed Catholics, then the Holy Spirit dwells within us. We need not go search for him, but we have to be courageous. Conversions happen because God works through our natural ability as humans to do the supernatural work of God. We have to choose to say yes to his grace. Turn to God in prayer and choose to say yes to the grace that God wants to give through us for the conversion of others.

The Lord of the universe is after each person who walks the earth. He wants to use very ordinary Christians to reach those persons. God can work through great speakers, big events, well-planned programs, and big budgets. But these things alone will not suffice. He needs faithfulness in his servants.

In other words, we won't reach the world by huddling in a parish event.

GOD MAKES HIMSELF PRESENT TO ME

I was very far from God when I started college. Looking back on it now, I consider it a low point in my life. I covered up my wounds and problems with alcohol, bravado, and chasing women. But God had a different plan for my life.

A group of Christians lived in my dorm. Half of them were Catholics and half were Baptists. They radiated joy and enjoyment of life. I couldn't help but be attracted to them because they lived life freely, unlike me. I was a slave to my passions, full of self-hatred, and I sought to escape reality in order to hide from it all.

They made God present to me by loving me right where I was. They probably did not even like me much. I was as rough as almost any nineteen-year-old I have ever known. But these young men led me to an encounter with Jesus that changed my life. I ended up going to confession, being freed of the burden that weighed me down, and then praying before the Blessed Sacrament the most sincere prayer of my life. I said, "Jesus, I am not sure what this means, but I give my life to you. I am yours."

Jesus is always present to us. Our job as evangelists is to make his presence known to others. In fact, God cannot fail to be present to all people because by his very nature he exists in all places. He is omnipresent. God is not only present, he also loves everyone unconditionally and is actively pursuing a relationship with each of us. Yet some are unaware of his loving presence. Therefore, it is our job to try to raise this awareness, make him known, and then be alongside others as they move into this awareness and relationship.

This is what happened to me. This is what the world needs.

This is why I wrote this book.

PETER

isn't a saint because he got it all right. In fact, he is a saint despite the fact that he got a whole lot wrong. That ought to be comforting for us who sometimes sin, often mess up, are always imperfect, and are not the best evangelists. Peter is not a model of success, if by success we mean high achievement. In fact, when he is mentioned in the Bible, he is frequently reactive, impetuous, and making mistakes. Peter is not highly educated. He is not abundantly gifted. He does not necessarily have the qualities of a great leader.

But the great thing about Peter is that he allows God to use him for big things, despite all of this. He humbles himself and returns to the Lord, even after he denies him. He then goes on to evangelize in some of the most amazing ways in the book of Acts. He preaches the first sermon after Pentecost, and the result is three thousand people are baptized! He performs miracles. He has an angel break him out of prison.

Peter was a fisherman by trade, and he lived in what was considered a backwater town. He had no wealth or prestige. Yet his name is still remembered because of the choices he made. This is because Peter allowed his heart to be slowly transformed from a fisherman into a fisher of men. His ultimate joy came in fulfilling the command of his master to make disciples.

Peter evangelized in a radically effective way, despite his limitations. We ought to find great comfort in taking Peter as an example of how to be a great evangelist. It is not about what we do but about how much we open up to the grace of God by constantly saying yes to divine grace.

QUESTIONS FOR CONSIDERATION

✳ *Why does the Catholic Church exist? Try to state the mission of the Church in your own words.*

✳ *What role do you play in the mission of the Church? Do you believe that your role is important?*

✳ *Have you ever intentionally tried to evangelize? How did it go?*

✳ *What barriers exist in your heart that prevent you from evangelizing?*

CHAPTER 2

THE STRATEGY OF JESUS

Jesus gave the Church a mission (to make disciples of all nations), a vision (to establish his kingdom as best we can in this life, until it is fully realized in heaven), and a strategy (to invest our lives deeply in a handful of disciples and then teach others to do the same). But how do we, as individuals and local groups, make the big shift to employ the strategy of Jesus? The first step is to realize that many of the strategies we currently use are no longer effective.

Not long ago, I heard a story from a great Catholic family who moved to a new city. When they registered at their new parish, no one called or emailed them to welcome them. Nobody came to visit them; nobody helped orient them to their new parish. All they got were instructions about how to make donations. This kind of welcome is in no way hospitable or effective. Can you imagine Jesus sending a donation form to someone who moved near him in Galilee? That was not how Jesus operated.

In addition, becoming a disciple of Jesus is not first and foremost behavior modification. If that were true, we could never be disciples, because no one on earth is without sin. But often our Catholic culture pushes behavior modification as the main goal of our faith. This is not to say it isn't necessary to love as Christ loves. But we need to flip the script.

BELONGING, BELIEVING, BEHAVING

Love requires us to reach out to others, loving them as God loves them. We should love them for who they are and where they are. We shouldn't demand they become the persons we wish they would be before we are willing to love them. Jesus does not begin loving someone after that person starts loving him. Jesus wants us to belong to him and have faith in him, and then our behavior should change for the better.

Our Lord actively sought relationships with people who were considered outsiders spiritually, morally, and socially. He became friendly with Pharisees, prostitutes, unscrupulous tax collectors, and others who were shunned by the "righteous." Indeed, he calls everyone to "repent, and believe" (Mark 1:15). But note, he does not require his disciples to be morally perfect in order to follow him. Throughout the Gospels, the disciples fail time and time again. If Christ had given up on them for their failures, then he would have had no disciples. Discipleship is a relationship, and relationships are a journey.

All good, sound relationships are journeys. When my wife and I were dating, first we built a friendship in a natural way. This is like the sense of belonging Jesus offered those he encountered. Later, as our friendship grew, my future wife and I decided we wanted to have a relationship with greater meaning based on mutual trust and faith in each other. This is like the faith Jesus asked from his disciples. My wife and I built the foundation of friendship and trust, then fell in love, and only then did we commit to marriage. This is like the change in behavior that comes with committing to Jesus.

Something similar happened in college during my conversion to Catholicism. I had some friends who loved me in spite of my sinfulness and problems. They allowed me to belong. After a time, they asked me to attend a retreat that changed my life. I had a conversion and made a decision to follow Christ. I began to have faith. Soon my choices changed for the better because I fell in love with Jesus. My behavior changed.

Jesus' parable of the one who sows the seeds breaks this open even further. The seed that the devil snatches symbolizes people who hear God's word but dismiss it. Such people never belong, have faith, or act differently.

The seed on the rocks grows fast but dies because it lacks roots. That example symbolizes people who merely seek the feel-good aspect of Christianity without living by God's laws. These people may change behavior for a long or short time, but they don't have genuine faith and don't deeply belong. Such cultural Catholics go through the motions of faith, but their hearts and actions have not conformed to being a disciple of Jesus.

The seed that lands in thorns is choked by the concerns of the world. People who are like that thorn-engulfed seed want life both ways, and that is impossible. They choose the world, not Jesus. They might seem to belong to him, but they don't. They don't believe, and they don't change their actions. They don't grow or bear fruit.

Finally, there is the seed that falls upon rich soil. It grows to a full harvest. Here, people not only belong to God, they fully believe what he says, and their behavior reflects their belonging and their beliefs. They start by being accepted in the good soil and are nurtured by strong Christians who help tend the new growth of faith. They then mature in community and faith. This is the way Jesus operated.

Belonging is an important first step. We all share a common dignity and are all loved by God. But we do not stop with mere relationships, because Christianity is far more than a club. Our goal is to love others as Jesus did. Jesus loved others enough to generously offer them something more than just a relationship and community. He wanted salvation for them and the world.

Therefore, we must eventually move from belonging to believing. Believing requires a change of heart, a conversion; therefore we have to be evangelists. Finally, we can challenge and encourage others to behave because they, too, have committed their lives to following Jesus. Love demands that we seek the good of the other. Love demands growth and transformation for those who follow Jesus.

THE POWER OF MATH

"Spiritual addition" is a term used in campus ministry. It means that one person can bring another to convert and become a disciple who follows Jesus. That is a moment to rejoice, but it is not a stopping point. Still, for most Catholic evangelists, bringing a person to conversion is considered a success. We try to find converts. That is good, but it is not enough. Simply making converts ourselves is not the bar Jesus wants us to leap over. That was not his strategy.

Another principle in campus ministry is this: what Jesus wants is "spiritual multiplication" rather than addition.[5]

When he started his ministry, Jesus sought and called fishermen to follow him to "fish" for men (see Matthew 4:19). Following was step one. Following makes a person a disciple. Then the person has to be formed into one who "fishes" for men, one who makes disciples. Jesus wants us to go even further and make disciple makers. That is spiritual multiplication. That is the way the Church changed the world in a few generations after Pentecost.

We could be great evangelists and preach to thousands, like St. Patrick, St. Paul, and St. Francis Xavier did. Moving the crowds as they did would be wonderful evangelization, but there is a better idea: choose a few people at a time, spend time and effort molding them, and form them to become makers of disciples. That is the process Jesus showed us. He devoted his time to making his twelve followers into fishers of men. Yes, he spoke to large crowds, but most of his focus was on the Twelve, who went out to make more fishers of men in their turn.[6]

In fact, Jesus spent about seventy-three percent of the time during his three years of ministry with twelve men. He deeply invested in them and taught them to do the same. Later on, St. Peter would invest in St. Mark, who would then write the Gospel we read today. St. John invested in St. Ignatius of Antioch, who became a bishop and martyr. The apostles went on to do with others what Jesus did with them. They invested in a handful of others and taught them to do the same.

This strategy works, and it can be proven mathematically. Here is a thought experiment from a campus ministry website: If you get a thousand folks a year to follow what you preach for twenty years, you'll have twenty thousand people following Christ.

But what if you follow a different strategy? Suppose three people find faith in Jesus through your witness, and you then personally mentor them. Suppose you form them into disciples so they evangelize and "disciple" three more. If all of those disciple makers evangelize three more, at the end of twenty years there will be millions of followers of Jesus! Spiritual multiplication is powerful—and that is what we are called to do. That is evangelization that is personal.[7]

If we want to hit our goal to "make disciples of all nations," our plan is spiritual multiplication. As Paul relates to Timothy, "What you have heard from me before many witnesses entrust to faithful men who will be able to teach others also" (2 Timothy 2:2).

WHAT ABOUT TODAY?

In many ways, the twenty-first-century Catholic Church has stopped operating through the strategy of Jesus. If we really believe that Jesus revealed how we ought to spread the gospel, then it is no wonder that we have seen a decline in many parts of the Church, at least in the global North and West. We cannot expect to fulfill the commandments of Jesus successfully without operating as Jesus showed us how to do.

At the parish level of ministry, we often see staff managing parish structures and programs. While much of this is necessary, we cannot be distracted from our primary call to relational ministry.

Rather than investing in a few and teaching them to do the same with others, most staff and key volunteers spend the bulk of their time running programs, handling administration, putting on events, teaching classes, and managing the parish operations. We spend the vast majority of time, money, and effort in things that keep us very busy, but are they bringing about the conversions and the change of the culture we are hoping they will? We can know we are successful by looking at the fruit or lack of fruit. For instance, how many people are being baptized? How many are moving toward a deeper relationship with God? How many disciples of Jesus are we making? If the answers are few to none, then we need to change how we operate or we will continue to decline.

REACTIVE OR PROACTIVE LEADERS

Many Catholics in leadership roles can profit by learning to be proactive. Catholic leaders who are *reactive*:

- Know our Church has problems that have to be solved.

- Focus on rapidly fixing these problems.

- Tackle daily issues and set aside matters of the big picture.

- Believe the culture is shattering our world and the Church.

- Are controlled by the force of the problems, taking no initiative on their own.

- Sit back and wait for renewal to happen instead of causing change.

- Stay busy with programs and plans that have few lasting good outcomes.

- Agree to too many tasks due to their lack of strategy and because they think doing something beats doing nothing.

- Tackle the most urgent problem instead of planning.

- Let others take the lead in doing something even when they know they should do it first.

On the contrary, Church leaders with a *proactive* approach:

- Know the Catholic Church has a mission and must live it out.

- Plan carefully to make that mission a reality.

- Establish a direction, see the big picture, and know how to stay on course every day.

- Accept that today's culture, with its good and bad points, is the mission field God gave us.

- Seek to understand problems before simply trying to fix them.

- Create a sense of purpose in the community with a vision others can and do embrace.

- Realize that renewing God's Church will take time, so actively devise plans and actions that can have long-lasting results.

- Choose actions with long-lasting outcomes, avoiding only fixing immediate problems.

- Say "no" a lot (in keeping with a long-term strategy).

- Select actions based on what is most important.

- Choose activities based on what is right, even if others are not interested.

Here is an example of an issue from both reactive and proactive points of view. If people miss Mass, it is probably because it is not something they consider to be very important. How do church leaders change people's minds? Reactive leaders will focus on the problem: folks not showing up at church. Reactive leaders are frustrated and maybe irritated. They think about strategies to attract people to Mass. They might see what worked at another parish and try it at their church. They might browse the internet for solutions. Or they might spend money on a new curriculum. In the end, they implement a lot of things that usually fail. Why? Bringing people back to church requires more than a new program that welcomes them back. People are not a problem to solve.

Catholic leaders who are proactive do not just address the symptoms: "Why are the pews not full every Sunday?" They don't simply ask how to convince people to come to Mass. Rather, the question is bigger: "How do I fulfill Jesus' Great Commission? How do I obey what our Lord commanded us to do?" In short, the vision is big, not small. Our goal is to make all people great saints and evangelists. That is huge. And because God is up to the task, so are we. Let us aim for heaven, holiness, and a relationship that is personal with Jesus and his Church. If we do that, problems will be solved, including attracting people to Mass.

But all Catholics must acknowledge our own failures. Sacraments, devotions, teachings, hierarchy, doctrine, and structure are not the problem. Our problem is our approach to these gifts of God. The problem lies in our vision, our strategy, and our lack of prayer, holiness, and accountability.

For too long the Church has depended on reactive leadership that has waited to respond to needs based on problems that surface. The Church desperately needs leaders who are proactive about doing the right thing the right way and allowing God to empower us to do it.

LOOK

at the issues that the Catholic Church is facing in your local parish and area. Many folks identify themselves as Catholics but do not go to church. Some who are baptized do not consider themselves Catholic anymore. Many are not aware that they can have a personal encounter (or relationship) with Jesus.

Now contrast those issues with the bigger issue that Jesus had to deal with. All of humanity needed to be saved. How would you solve this problem? Would you start a worldwide ministry that could reach as many as possible? Maybe an internet video channel or a podcast? Would you use social media or start a TV show? Maybe you would write or publish books.

That's not the way Jesus approached it.

Jesus lived among us for thirty-three years. Thirty of those years we know little about, but we can guess they were spent in preparation for his active ministry. He spent about three years actively ministering to the world, revealing the plan of salvation and the nature of God's love to us and showing us how we ought to pass on his grace to the world. He did this by investing the vast majority of his time, effort, teaching, and love in a small handful of men. He then told them to do with others what he did for them.

He aimed deep and narrow. Our modern strategy is generally shallow and wide. He aimed mostly at individuals. We aim mostly at crowds. He wanted converted hearts, intimacy, and accountability. We settle for so much less. Jesus wanted multiplication of disciples. At best, we go for addition.

Our modern strategy has failed us because we have tried to rely on our own methodology. It is time to return to the strategy of Jesus.

QUESTIONS FOR CONSIDERATION

✳ *Who are you intentionally trying to invest in?*
Do you give them enough time, care, and effort?
Do they know that you care for each of them as a person and not just as a project?

✳ *Who do you lead? Besides those you have authority over, who are the people following you because they want to? Do they know where all of you are headed? If those following you do not know, you are not leading. You are managing. The Church needs you to lead.*

✳ *Who do you follow? You have to know who you listen to. Who is your mentor? This is not about listening to a speaker, reading something (including this book), or even following Jesus. It is about real friends you trust and choose to follow as they show you the way. Do they know what makes you tick? Are you close to them? Most importantly, are they following a plan to form you into a great saint and a great evangelist? No? Then you are not being led properly.*

✳ *Where are you headed? If you do not know, you cannot measure success. What strategy defines and guides your mission? Do you know what works in evangelization? Do you want to do what Jesus did?*

✳ *When you have a destination, how will you get there? What plan of action will you put in play to get you there? If you don't know, keep reading. That is what this book is all about.*

CHAPTER 3

WHERE ARE THEY AND WHERE DO THEY NEED TO GO?

The map inside my brain works fairly well. If I feel I know where I am headed, I usually do not use a map or a phone to guide me. Sometimes I miss a turn or get lost and have to ask for help, though. I could avoid that if I use the tools that are readily available. Discipleship can work in a similar way. We may think we know where we are headed, so we often fail to ask for help. That can result in getting lost on our journey.

Furthermore, in order to better help others grow closer to Jesus and the Catholic Church, we will need to know where they currently are spiritually and what they need to move forward. Even though I know this is true, sometimes I am tempted to fill in the blanks of someone's story. My guess is that we all do the same thing, to some extent. Let's test my theory.

What comes to mind when I tell you that I was "raised Catholic"? Do you think of my family praying together, attending Mass, and going to confession? For many families, that would be accurate. But to be "raised Catholic" means different things to different people. It could mean being raised like St. Thérèse of Lisieux, whose parents were both canonized by the Church, too! She always had a close relationship with Jesus and his Church. Or, someone who describes himself as being "raised Catholic" might mean that his grandmother was a Catholic and he went to church a few times as a kid, though he was not even baptized.

If we assume we know someone's story, we will not know what that person needs to grow.

STEPS TO SUCCESS

The first step is figuring out where someone is on his or her spiritual journey. Sherry Weddell did the Church a great favor in her landmark book *Forming Intentional Disciples*.[8] In this book she gave us a starting point for assessing where someone is by describing the different steps, or thresholds, most of us go through before becoming disciples of Jesus. She identified five of them:

1. **Trust** – when a person experiences Christianity or a Catholic in an affirmative way

2. **Curiosity** – when Christianity strikes someone as thought-provoking and the person is interested in learning

3. **Openness** – when someone is willing to consider the transformation that comes about by being a disciple of Jesus

4. **Seeking** – when someone steps out to search for Jesus and respond to him

5. **Intentional Discipleship** – when one becomes a disciple by intentionally choosing to walk in Jesus' way

Weddell estimates that the vast majority of Catholics are not yet intentional disciples of Jesus. They may be involved, serve, participate, and pray, yet they have not consciously been converted to discipleship. This highlights the crux of our issue. Most Catholics need to be converted to Jesus Christ. This includes many clergy, religious, and lay leaders. We cannot judge discipleship by mere outward activity but rather by whether someone has intentionally chosen a life that follows Jesus.

WHAT NEXT?

The goals of following Jesus are to get to heaven, take as many others with us as we can, be a saint on the way, and glorify God through it all. We can't be OK with being OK Catholics. Neither should we be OK with just making disciples. We have to go further to make holy and fruitful disciples who go on to do the same with others.

To help conceptualize the big picture of what a Catholic disciple is meant to be, I propose using a tool I call a discipleship pathway. I believe this tool is powerful. I have shared it with many leaders, including in a webinar. Before I share it here, I have some suggested guidelines:

1. Never put anyone in a box. When assessing
    yourself and other people, avoid labels. Everyone
    is unique. No one fits a label or our preconceived
    notions all the time. Get to know the other
    person so you have a better idea of what he or
    she needs to live and grow in a life of faith.

2. My suggestions are conceptual only. Most of
    us will not fit exactly into any one area. So
    when you work through my suggested
    discipleship guidelines, remember that particular
    people may have a spiritual characteristic in one
    area, a moral characteristic in another, and
    another in evangelization and in mission.

3. Everyone starts somewhere. After assessing the
    guidelines, if you begin to assign yourself a place
    where you wish you were not, don't be
    discouraged. You are not in a competition.
    Use your own starting point as your place
    to begin to grow as a disciple. God knows
    where you are and wants you to grow. The
    end matters more than the beginning.

4. Avoid assuming that a person's church activity,
    prayer habits, or service makes him or her an
    intentional disciple. Intention is the key
    difference between a disciple and one who is not.
    Has the person really said yes to Jesus' call?

THE DISCIPLESHIP PATHWAY – STAGES OF DISCIPLESHIP

The point of the following pathway is to help conceptualize the vision of a disciple and what the needs are at different stages.

Being a Pre-disciple

This includes Sherry Weddell's first four thresholds of conversion (trust, curiosity, openness, and seeking). At this stage the goal is to help the pre-disciple become a disciple of Jesus.

Markers:

1. Jesus is not part of my spiritual life.

2. I have never made a choice to place Jesus at the center of my life.

3. I may have been taught about the Faith and received all the sacraments, but I have not been evangelized.

Needs:

1. I need Jesus' gospel message of salvation to be presented to me clearly, and I need a chance to respond.

2. I need a first-time conversion to Jesus, and I must invite him into my heart to be my Lord and Savior.

3. I need friendship with a disciple of Jesus who can evangelize me and accompany me.

Being a Developing Disciple

Markers:

1. I have only a little knowledge of a Christian lifestyle and Catholic teaching.

2. I have begun to pray every day, and I want to be free of sin by going to confession and turning away from vices.

3. I regularly receive the sacraments, especially Holy Communion and confession.

4. I still lean toward a me-focused spiritual life.

5. I am starting to try to be active in evangelization but mostly limit myself to activities I think are easy, such as participating in parish programs or talking to those who approach me.

6. I serve once in a while but more regularly. My heart is beginning to do so for love of God and others.

7. I have begun to recognize spiritual gifts and charisms (gifts of the Holy Spirit given for the good of the community) and possibly use them.

8. I am leading others in the religious community.

Needs:

1. I need help and accountability from mature disciples or peers to continue to grow in intimacy with Jesus.

2. I need further catechetical formation.

3. I need guidance in overcoming the gaps in the moral life.

4. I need clarity on how to be a better evangelist and how to bring someone to conversion effectively.

5. I need to look to the Church's big picture and its mission to guide me.

Being an Intentional Disciple

Markers:

1. My attitude toward Jesus and the Church is positive.

2. I have accepted Jesus as my Lord and Savior and, with intention, I have decided to follow him and place him at the center of my life.

3. I am still ignorant of what the life of a disciple looks like.

4. I still have a mostly me-focused spiritual life, which shows signs of spiritual immaturity.

5. I feel excited to talk to others about our Lord but usually only when I feel the time is right.

6. I serve when I feel obligated or have a sense of zeal. I rely on feelings and mood too often.

Needs:

1. I need mentoring in order to follow Jesus, with time given to me by more mature disciples (at least one) who help hold me accountable.

2. I need help to pray and become familiar with Sacred Scripture.

3. I need systematic and ongoing catechetical formation.

4. I need guidance in the moral life.

5. I require basic formation in the characteristics of what being a disciple of Jesus means.

6. I need clarity on the goal of the life of a disciple—that there is more God wants from me.

Being a Missionary Disciple

Markers:

1. I am doing more to be an active evangelist, and I am able to make disciples, but I am not capable of multiplying disciples.

2. I take the initiative to seek my own formation and growth.

3. I have a regular and intimate daily prayer life.

4. I continually grow in catechesis, and the gaps in my knowledge are becoming smaller.

5. I have a full sacramental life.

6. I am moving toward being spirituality centered on others and God.

7. I understand my spiritual gifts and charisms and more consistently serve through them.

8. I am considered an exceptional and rare Catholic.

Needs:

1. I need in-depth catechesis and formation in my interior life.

2. I need to be held accountable for evangelization and mission.

3. I need ongoing building up and advice.

4. I need to create for myself opportunities to evangelize and the freedom to take on service.

5. I need to begin to multiply disciples—form disciples who make other disciples.

6. I need opportunities to mentor less-mature disciples and nondisciples.

Being a Multiplier Disciple

Markers:

1. Sacraments are indispensable to me.

2. I pray daily, and it is personal, intense, deep, and fruitful.

3. I am deeply knowledgeable about doctrine and how to hand on the Faith to others.

4. Most of my time is spent in service to others. I humbly love God through a life centered on God and others.

5. I help others work through my gifts and charisms.

6. I am a fruitful spiritual leader in most relationships.

7.   I am mentoring others who do the same.
     Thus, I am spiritually multiplying.

Needs:

1.   I need to continue to dive deeper with Jesus
     through catechesis, prayer, the sacraments,
     growth in virtue, etc.

2.   I need ongoing deep spiritual formation from a
     holy spiritual director or mentor.

3.   I need to continue to find situations and relationships
     where I can evangelize and form others.

4.   I need to have consistent and intentional
     relationships where I am the spiritual mentor
     and others are my apprentices.

5.   I need to be held accountable and to be in
     community, but in most Christian relationships,
     I am a leader.

All people, regardless of where they are, need ongoing healing, especially in the sacrament of confession. Others might need more specialized healing, including help breaking addictions or overcoming mental health issues. Regardless, Jesus came to preach, save, and heal. Therefore, we need to seek out healing ourselves and also help others wherever they might need healing.

Furthermore, remember that these are merely ways of conceptualizing where someone is on the path of discipleship. Rarely does someone fit every marker or experience every need in a particular category. Most will have markers in two or more stages, which means the corresponding needs will run up and down the categories.

ASSESS WHERE YOU ARE

Start by assessing where you are in the stages of discipleship and what your needs are. If you are not a disciple yet, then seek out conversion or make an act of faith now. We need not be worried about formulas. The point is to seek a relationship with Jesus in an intentional movement of our heart, mind, and soul—where we place our faith in Jesus and make him the Lord and Savior of our lives.

If you find that you are struggling in a particular area, then try to find help. One of the biggest difficulties many disciples have is finding others to help them. I understand. Do not give up your search for friendships that are based on following Jesus. In fact, it sometimes means we have to lead with vulnerability and merely express this desire to others, who may also share it but have not voiced it either.

The next step is to use the stages to understand better where others are and what they need. I have a chart of these stages that I sometimes show to others whom I am mentoring or "discipling." I explain the different stages and ask them to give me their best assessment of themselves. Almost all of them have an accurate idea of where they are. Then we formulate a plan, based on what they need to grow, and we start to meet together to walk further down the road with Jesus.

The stages are clearly not a quick fix. In fact, our job is not to fix anyone. Rather, we are supposed to accompany others intentionally while we, too, have them walk with us. But we should always remember that the Holy Spirit is the true leader of all disciples.

SAMARITANS

were considered heretics by the Jews of Jesus' time. In fact, most Jews who were traveling from Galilee to Judea (or vice versa) would avoid Samaria altogether so as to avoid contact with Samaritans. This is why the parable of the "good Samaritan" was probably offensive to some Jews. It was also why the apostles were stunned to find Jesus talking to a Samaritan at a well. To make it worse, this was a woman, and it was rare for a Jewish man to talk to a woman all by himself in public.

Clearly, this is an exceptional conversation. Jesus goes out of his way to break several societal norms in order to encounter this woman and evangelize her. Jesus first asks her to give him a drink of water. She responds that it is an incredible request because of the rift between Jews and Samaritans. Jesus then uses the opportunity to talk about the woman's deepest desires to be saved from her sin.

Throughout the conversation, we see the woman's faith in Jesus begin to flower. Jesus properly assesses where the woman is (pre-disciple), evangelizes her by preaching Good News, and then invites her to accept him as the Messiah. She does. In her excitement, she cannot help but run off and tell the whole town what has happened.

What about you and me? We, too, have the opportunity to have daily encounters with Jesus, be converted, and go out and tell others. Where are you on your journey, and where do you want to go? Maybe it is time to allow Jesus to sit by you and help examine your heart.

QUESTIONS FOR CONSIDERATION

✳ *Spend a few minutes reviewing the different thresholds and stages of discipleship. Where would you place yourself?*

✳ *Where have you become stagnant or need further growth? What are your own needs?*

✳ *Do you believe Jesus wants more from you?*

✳ *If you are not a disciple, spend some time in prayer, placing Jesus at the center of your life.*

✳ *If you are a disciple, then write down three goals you have for further growth. Who can you share these goals with?*

✳ *Think of someone you know who may need to be evangelized. What kind of needs do you think they may have? How might you help them?*

CHAPTER 4

BIG QUESTIONS
AND OPEN HEARTS

I have a good friend who is a great evangelist. One of the things I admire about him is his approachable nature. He is easy to get along with. But in addition to merely being nice, he does not waste much time with small talk. This is because he wants to get beyond the fluff and find out what really makes you tick. Maybe this is why I like him so much. We can't be around each other for very long and merely chitchat. We talk about things that matter, and it makes a huge difference in both our lives.

One of the conversational techniques I have learned from our friendship is how to show a genuine interest in the other person. It starts by being curious about that person. This is not a superficial show of curiosity but real curiosity that flows out of sincerely wanting to know what matters in the other person's life. This curiosity requires asking a lot of questions—the kind of questions that matter.

We all know that everyone likes to be valued and heard. But many aspiring Catholic evangelists talk too much. Rarely do people who are distant from God or the Catholic

Church like to hear a monologue about faith, especially when they do not first feel cared for. Most modern folks are not asking questions about purgatory or Mary but rather are concerned with self-identity, meaning, and God's existence. This is why the best evangelists know how to ask big questions and practice listening, friendship, and long-term prayer. The point of valuing others and having deep conversations with them is to win the right to be heard and thus move them into active evangelization.

BIG QUESTIONS MATTER

In our evangelization efforts, we should ask more questions than the person we are with. Asking questions can help us achieve several goals of relationship building. First, it shows that we are interested in the other person— his or her values, thoughts, and so on. Second, asking questions gets others talking about themselves, and we can understand their viewpoint better. We then are able to serve them better and move them forward. Third, questions are a great way to start a conversation, keep a conversation moving, or take a conversation to a much deeper level.

Here are some sample questions I have found to be helpful in various situations. Not every question is right for all times in a person's life, so be discerning about choosing which questions to ask when.

Questions about life's meaning and purpose and about identity:

- Where did human beings come from?

- In your life, where do you find meaning?

- Where do you think power comes from?

- Define success and give examples.

- Do you have a destiny, and if so, what is it?
  How do you know?

- What gives your life meaning?

Questions on truth, untruths, priorities, and values:

- How can you be sure of what is true and what is not?

- Are you willing to give your life for anything?
  If so, for what?

- State your highest priorities. How did you decide
  on them?

- Tell me the things or people you are passionate about.
  What issues do you argue for or against, and why?

- What people or things strongly influence or
  motivate you? What are your dreams for life?

- What do you hope to achieve in life?

- When you describe yourself as _____,
  what do you mean?

Questions about how to live and act and about what is right and wrong:

- How can you be sure of what is right and
  what is wrong?

- How do you decide how you should act?

- Are there human rights that are universal? If so, what are they, and how are such rights determined?

- In a moral sense, are some acts relative?

- Is anything one hundred percent moral or immoral all the time?

- Where do the problems of human beings and societies come from? Where does evil come from?

- Can evil be eliminated? How can the problems of human society be solved?

This is not the only way to categorize such questions. Another path is to understand the labels people give themselves and others and ask a lot of questions to get past them and see the person, not the label. A person's story must replace whatever label is applied to him or her. Labels can help start a conversation, but a label is only a beginning.

Questions for atheists, agnostics, "nones," the unchurched (nonbelievers):

- Tell me about the God you don't believe in.

- Describe what is most fulfilling about being _____.

- If you describe God to others, what do you say?

- What, if anything, do you know about Jesus?

- In your view, what does Christianity contribute to others' lives?

- Do you believe any kind of higher power exists? If so, can you describe this power for me? If not, can you tell me why not?

- Have you ever believed in God? If so, why did you stop?

- If you decided to believe in a god, can you describe such a power?

Questions for those in other religions (Hindus, Muslims, Mormons, etc.):

- If you pray, how do you pray? Can you tell me about prayer?

- What do you find most fulfilling about being _____, and can you describe why?

- How do you describe the god you worship?

- Tell me what you know about Jesus.

- Does anything about Christianity appeal to you?

Questions for non-Catholic Christians:

- Describe what you believe about Jesus.

- Do you practice your faith every day? If so, how?

- Describe your relationship with Jesus.

- Do you find anything appealing about Catholicism?

- Tell me what you know about the Catholic Church.

Questions for Catholics:

- In your own experience, describe what it means to be Catholic.

- Do you take time to pray? How do you pray?

- Do you have a personal relationship with God?

- Has there ever been a time when you felt especially
  close to Jesus? If so, describe it. If not, have you
  wanted to feel close to him?

UNDERSTANDING VERSUS ACCEPTANCE

Understanding does not mean acceptance. Merely
knowing what someone believes, understanding where
someone is coming from, or learning about a belief system
does not mean accepting any part of it. Furthermore,
accepting the person does not mean accepting all that
the person thinks, feels, and believes.

St. James tells us to "be quick to hear, slow to speak,
slow to anger" (James 1:19). Yet, if you are like me, you
might operate in the opposite manner at times. I can
be slow to listen, quick to speak, and quick to anger. I
sometimes want to win an argument, get others to agree
with me, or prove them wrong. Yet how detrimental this
is to evangelizing others!

I sometimes operate from the assumption that I already
understand where someone is coming from. But making
assumptions is never wise. It is as if I am in Oz, still looking
for the great and powerful wizard (the right argument)
that will give me all the power I need to have a successful
outcome. When I pull back the curtain and discover that
the other person wants to be valued, welcomed, loved, and
in relationship with others, I am a much better evangelist.
It is during these times of discovery that I allow the Holy
Spirit to lead the way.

I then can stop trying to win an argument or prove others wrong. Instead I am able to love them enough to meet them where they are, so that I can possibly lead them to somewhere better.

IN CONVERSATION

I have had the opportunity to evangelize in various situations. Here is a sampling from an amalgamation of several conversations I have had through the years, which I hope will give you a sense of how you might have your own conversations.

For a bit of background, the hypothetical person I am talking to is a fallen-away Catholic who is on the threshold of openness, but I don't know this yet and am trying to evaluate where he is. We met because our kids play sports together. We really enjoy each other's company, and when this person found out I was Catholic (because I intentionally mentioned that fact in other conversations), he said he was Catholic, too, but didn't go to church anymore. I told him I would love to talk more about the Church if he ever wanted to do so. He took me up on the invitation, and we met at a coffee shop the following week. We have already gone through the initial conversational small talk.

Me – *So, when you emailed me, you said you had some questions about getting more involved in the Church. I would love to talk about those, but if you don't mind, can I ask you some questions first?*

Fallen-away Catholic (FAC) – *I don't mind at all.*

Me – *Great. Would you tell me a little about your religious background? Were you raised as a Catholic, and if so, what did that look like in your family?*

FAC – *My parents were both Catholic, so I was baptized as a baby. But later on my dad stopped going, even though the rest of us continued to attend Mass. By the time I was nine or ten, we all stopped going, except on Easter and Christmas. Since I left for college, I've only been to Mass a few times—mostly during the holidays when my wife wants us all to go, because it seems like the right thing for us to do.*

Me – *Was your experience of the Catholic Church generally a positive thing?*

FAC – *I guess it was mostly positive. Of course, as a kid, I thought Mass was pretty boring. I still don't really understand everything that is going on there.*

Me – *I bet you're in the majority there. Many who go to Mass every week don't understand it all, and that is unfortunate. Do you still feel any connection to a Catholic identity? Do you still call yourself a Catholic?*

FAC – *Oh, yeah. I am not an "active" Catholic, but I would still say I'm Catholic.*

Me – *Would you say you are a spiritual person? Do you pray?*

FAC – *I would say I'm somewhat spiritual. I pray, but not very regularly. I mean, I'll say something to God once in a while, but I don't sit down and read the Bible every day, if that's what you mean.*

Me – *I was just wondering what kind of spiritual connection you might still have to God.*

FAC – *Well, I certainly believe God is real. We had to come from somewhere.*

Me – *Do you believe God is personal?*

FAC – *I'm not sure what you mean by that ...*

Me – *Well, do you believe God knows you, cares for you, loves you, has a plan for your life? Things like that.*

FAC – *I'm not sure. I've never really thought of God like that.*

Me – *If you had to describe God, what would you say?*

FAC – *Maybe like what you see in the old paintings. An old man with a big gray beard. Someone that's in heaven and knows everything.*

Me – *So, not so much a loving and personal God?*

FAC – *Maybe not so much.*

Me – *What about Jesus? Would you mind telling me about what you know about him?*

FAC – *Probably not that much. I know he is the Son of God. He is the one all the Bible stories are about. Stuff like that.*

Me – *I really do appreciate you taking the time to answer all my questions. I'm just naturally curious about where people are coming from.*

FAC – *Sure.*

Me – *So, what were those questions you wanted to talk about with me?*

ASSESSMENT

From this conversation, I can tell that my friend struggles to see God as a personal God. His false concept is actually held by many Catholics![9] This means that one of our first steps is introducing God as someone who truly cares about us and wants to have a relationship with us. My goal would be to continue to build the relationship until I start to see signs of openness to hearing the claims of Jesus and the Catholic Church. But first we have to work more on the understanding that God is personal. With that in mind, let's explore what that means more deeply.

When we speak about a personal relationship with God, we need to define what we mean clearly. It is a phrase that comes with some baggage. Some people argue that the phrase comes from Protestants and means nothing because it is relativistic. They may also state that it misses the communal part of being Christian. Other Catholics use the term a lot because they believe it pinpoints a piece of Catholicism that previous generations have not emphasized enough, if at all.

Both have a point. A personal relationship with Jesus cannot happen on our terms, only on Jesus' terms. The *Catechism of the Catholic Church* states:

> By faith, man completely submits his intellect and his will to God. With his whole being man gives his assent to God the revealer. Sacred Scripture calls this human response to God, the author of revelation, "the obedience of faith." (CCC 143)

Submission means there cannot be any relativism, and it means that the relationship's purpose is that we will be formed more into the image and the likeness of Jesus. We need not fear relativism will take hold as long as we submit. Further, we cannot simply say we have a one-on-one relationship with Jesus and be done. This is not a choice between Jesus and the Catholic Church. It is a relationship with both our Lord and his Church. That means we need the body of Christ—a community.

Sadly, Catholics have neglected their personal response to their faith. Thus, we should not neglect that personal aspect that is crucial to our being Catholic Christians.

With that as a backdrop, I wish to propose how we can have a personal relationship with both Jesus and the Church. When I dated my wife, time spent with her was paramount. Why? Because I wanted to know her as well as I could in a personal way. What did she like and not like? What were her passions, her pet peeves? I thirsted for knowledge of all things about her. Above all, though, I had to find out how to make choices that demonstrated my love to her.

When we love someone, we want to be as close and intimate as we can appropriately be. As Christians, we are called to have a close, intimate relationship with Jesus. But a lot of us do not know exactly what this means. Many of us are not sure how to have a meaningful relationship with Jesus. Actually, it is simple.

In all relationships, we decide how close we wish to be. After we reach a certain age, we decide what we want our faith to look like. No one, including the Church, can believe for us. Many of us settle for a relationship with God that is intellectual or emotional—not personal, chosen in faith. But knowing about Jesus or feeling good about him is not enough. After all, even demons know about Jesus. And all people have days when they do not feel good about him and what being his disciple demands. There are times we would rather not take up our crosses.

Those are precisely the reasons why, for our own spiritual good, we have to choose Jesus. We do this through an act of our heart and our will. And because faith is a response to grace, saying yes to Jesus can only happen because God chose us first.

Once we consciously and fully choose Jesus in faith, we have to do so over and over. This relationship in faith with our Lord is manifested mostly in prayer, receiving the sacraments, maturing in virtue as we love God and others, living in community, serving our fellow people, and helping others know, serve, follow, and love God. We are servants to Jesus, the King. As he commanded, we are called to love and serve him and others. We do this in the Church.

The idea of having a personal relationship with Jesus is too "Protestant" for some Catholics, but that perception is not accurate. Catholics today and for centuries have spoken of the importance of a personal relationship with Jesus. Just look at a few quotations from recent popes, the *Catechism*, and Vatican II:

> Being a Christian means having *a living relationship with the person of Jesus; it means putting on Christ, being conformed to him.*[10] (Pope Francis)

> Christian faith is not only a matter of believing that certain things are true, but above all a personal relationship with Jesus Christ.[11] (Pope Benedict XVI)

> This mystery [of faith], then, requires that the faithful believe in it, that they celebrate it, and that they live from it in a vital and personal relationship with the living and true God. This relationship is prayer. (CCC 2558)

> This conversion must be taken as an initial one, yet sufficient to make a man realize that he has been snatched away from sin and led into the mystery of God's love, who called him to enter into a personal relationship with Him in Christ. For, by the workings of divine grace, the new convert sets out on a spiritual journey, by means of which, already sharing through faith in the mystery of Christ's Death and Resurrection, he passes from the old man to the new one, perfected in Christ.[12] (Vatican II)

That is just a slice of the many powerful statements from the Church about our personal relationship with Jesus, so we should strive to develop it. Look at it like this. When we do the following things in faith and love, we are aiming to engage with Jesus personally:

- Pray every day.

- Attend Mass.

- Receive the sacrament of confession.

- Read Scripture.

- Act virtuously.

- Be merciful and kind.

- Share our faith with people.

In our wedding vows, when I promised to love my wife, my promise was not just an emotional act or something I did because I knew her well. No. I made a choice to love her, and every day in every way I decide to love her again, I reaffirm my commitment.

It is similar in my relationship with Jesus. To quote Thomas à Kempis,

> You cannot live well without a friend, and if Jesus be not your friend above all else, you will be very sad and desolate. Thus, you are acting foolishly if you trust or rejoice in any other. Choose the opposition of the whole world rather than offend Jesus. Of all those who are dear to you, let Him be your special love. Let all things be loved for the sake of Jesus, but Jesus for His own sake.
>
> Jesus Christ must be loved alone with a special love for He alone, of all friends, is good and faithful. For Him and in Him you must love friends and foes alike, and pray to Him that all may know and love Him.[13]

An intimate, personal relationship with Jesus can never happen by accident. This relationship is a choice. It's intentional. And it cannot take place without a community or, importantly, unless it's on Jesus' terms. Let us commit to building our personal relationship with Jesus *and* his Catholic Church.

THOSE AROUND US

Everyone around us has labels they apply to themselves. Doctor. Student. Former Catholic. Fallen-away Catholic. Conservative. Progressive. Atheist. Nothing. Jew. Muslim. Gay.

Many of these labels need an explanation before we can truly understand what is behind them. In order to be better evangelists, we need to stop filling in the gaps and instead allow ourselves to really *hear* the stories of those with whom we are speaking. We do not know what someone believes until we get to know the person beyond the labels. Another strategy we employ deals with the language we use.

If I tell an unchurched atheist that my peace came from a transformation in confession and then in prayer in front of a tabernacle, I might as well be speaking Aramaic. The words will not be understood in the same way that I understand them, and that is a problem. As is the case with any group of people, we Catholics have our own vocabulary and language to describe our unique practices, but this language is not universally used or understood. Thus, we have to learn to tailor our use of language to our audience.

With Hindus, I might talk about their idea of a higher power, but they will be ignorant of Sacred Scripture. With Baptists, I might use verses from the Bible because they accept the Bible as authoritative. With atheists, I will not constantly refer to Catholic sources, since they reject the authority of those sources.

We need to be evangelists who are discerning, comfortable with change, and adaptable to various people and situations. There is no formula that works for transforming hearts. But grace and our authentic love for others can do what formulas cannot.

THE RELATIONSHIP

between Jesus and Nicodemus is an interesting one because we see growth in the relationship throughout the Gospel of John. In John 3, we hear that Nicodemus is a Pharisee and part of the Sanhedrin (the Jewish ruling council). When we first meet Nicodemus, he approaches Jesus in the night because he is afraid of others finding out he wants to know more about Jesus. They enter into a conversation about being born again. Nicodemus seems curious about the claims he has heard about Jesus and therefore would like to have answers. Jesus not only answers his questions but also asks some of his own. He also challenges Nicodemus to believe in him.

The next time we see Nicodemus (John 7), there is a debate in the Sanhedrin about Jesus. The officials sent their guards to arrest Jesus, but they came back empty-handed because they were afraid of the crowds that followed him. The guards raise doubts against the idea that Jesus is evil; they are impressed by the things he says. Nicodemus appeals to Jewish law and says that Jesus has a right to defend himself. Here he is more than curious and is now openly seeking.

Finally, we have Nicodemus at the Cross (John 19). Jesus has died, and Nicodemus comes with Joseph of Arimathea to ask Pilate for the body of Jesus. He also brings with him all the necessary aloes and spices to bury the body. This would have cost him a considerable amount. At this point, we can surmise that he is a disciple of Jesus and has chosen to put Jesus at the center of his life.

QUESTIONS FOR CONSIDERATION

✳ *Reread the questions in the sample conversation in this chapter. Which ones challenge you the most?*

✳ *Think of someone you would like to evangelize. What questions would you like to ask that person?*

✳ *How comfortable do you feel about having
conversations that center on asking others questions
about their faith?*

✳ *Have you ever tried to win an argument about faith
issues? How did it turn out?*

CHAPTER 5

WHAT IS CONVERSION?

Few people read the legal jargon that comes with electronics. Even if they do slog through it all, do they understand it? Probably not, but they likely still say they read and concurred with the purchase conditions. This halfhearted, half-awake consent is the kind that often happens for Catholics at Mass. When it is time to state our beliefs by saying the Creed aloud, do we go through the motions or say it because we mean it? Without consent, does stating beliefs do any spiritual good? Can conversion take place without consent?

No, it cannot. To convert we must give our permission. Unlike checking the yes box on some routine terms and conditions, we must give our will and heart to conversion.

TO BE CONVERTED

Converting means changing, transforming, turning around. In the life of a Christian, this means turning away from sin, death, evil, and hell to seek grace, goodness, virtue, heaven, and a life of a disciple. Conversion is the transformation of our heart by an act of God's grace, to which we give our consent.

As a result, we call people who become Catholic *converts*, meaning they have embraced Catholicism as their faith and turned from prior beliefs. Many people who are most enthusiastic about Catholicism are converts, even coming from no faith. Why do they feel and act so vibrant? The reason is they had to make a conscious consent to become Catholic. That assent made all the difference. Consent means saying yes to the invitation from Jesus. It is an intentional act, by which we give permission for grace to transform us.

Here is the order in which conversion is described in Scripture:

1. People encounter Jesus.

2. They are invited to have a relationship with Jesus.

3. They assent to be in that relationship with Jesus.

4. They embark upon discipleship and mission.

Another way to say this is to state that people cannot be disciples and accomplish his mission until they consent to believe in Jesus and follow him. They cannot give consent until Jesus has graced them with an invitation (and the people have to know what they are assenting to). And they cannot receive an invitation from Jesus until they have encountered him.

When it comes to Catholic evangelization, we often behave like conversions will somehow just take place if we are good Catholics and put good programs out there. That is usually wishful thinking, proven by the fact that we have not seen widespread conversions while operating in this manner.

In addition, while grace from God always comes first, God's grace cannot work without our consent. There is no magic to it. If I were a wizard and used magic, it would do what I wanted as long as I said the right incantation and waved my wand the right way. This is not how grace works. Without consent, it will not bring us to faith. We who have the ability to choose must give our yes before we can be changed. Pay attention to the consent in these conversion stories.

St. Andrew's Conversion (John 1:35-42)

1.   Andrew, following John the Baptist, meets Jesus after John points him out.

2.   Jesus invites this future disciple to see where he is staying.

3.   Andrew consents to Jesus' invitation and begins following him.

4.   Andrew fetches his brother, Peter, to come and see Jesus because Andrew believes he has found the Messiah.

The Conversion of the Samaritan Woman by the Well (John 4:1-42)

1.   At a well in Samaria, a woman is drawing water and encounters Jesus.

2.   She hears Jesus' invitation to her to drink the water of eternal life and worship in "spirit and truth," opening the door to a relationship.

3. The woman believes and asks Jesus if she can drink the water.

4. She goes to the town—one that has shunned her—and tells people Jesus is the Messiah.

St. Peter's Reconversion (John 21:15-19)

1. Peter, who has denied Jesus three times, encounters his risen Lord on the beach.

2. Jesus invites his disciple to commit again by stating his love for Jesus three times.

3. Peter does state he loves Jesus, even if his love is imperfect.

4. After Jesus' ascension, Peter leads the Church.

The Three Thousand Conversions at Pentecost (Acts 2:14-47)

1. Peter, his soul filled with the promised Holy Spirit, proclaims Jesus' gospel in the streets.

2. Crowds hear the invitation to accept Jesus with faith as their Lord and Savior, repent of their sins, and experience the new joy through baptism.

3. Repentance is expressed by three thousand, who now believe in Jesus and are baptized.

4. The process of mission and discipleship starts in these new converts, and the Church grows.

There are numerous other examples. The process of evangelization that leads to conversion and mission is summed up by this continuum.

WHAT ABOUT TODAY?

Does this concept of consent work in Catholic ministry today? It must directly affect how we evangelize other people. These are some things to remember:

The actions of God come first: Always know that God cares for us and wants the salvation of the world more than we ever could. He has the heart of a perfect Father, and he pursues all of us. He works to bring everyone to himself. God is present always, everywhere. We have to show his presence to others so they can respond to him.

Some Catholics, said St. John Paul II, "only have the capacity to believe placed within them by Baptism and the presence of the Holy Spirit."[14] Note that grace has been given (capacity), but these Catholics have not given their consent to it, so it cannot operate fully within them. They have not yet had an initial conversion to Jesus. God waits for us to say yes before his grace can transform us. The salvation of the entire world began with Mary saying yes to the Holy Spirit at the Annunciation. That same Holy Spirit awaits each person's yes in order to save that person as well.

There are many forms of encounters with God: We can encounter him via our Christian witness, through proclamation of the *kerygma* (the gospel message that we will cover in-depth in the next chapter), Adoration of the Blessed Sacrament, our personal prayer, all the sacraments, and more. Encountering God is not limited to a program, class, or place. God cannot be tamed. When we invite people into a relationship with our Lord, we must be clear. In the Book of Acts, note that all conversions are preceded by an outright proclaiming of the gospel that is followed by a clear action plan: seek forgiveness, believe, and get baptized. Today, we also must be clear and forthright. To quote St. Paul:

> For, "every one who calls upon the name of the Lord will be saved." But how are men to call upon him in whom they have not believed? And how are they to believe in him of whom they have never heard? And how are they to hear without a preacher? And how can men preach unless they are sent? As it is written, "How beautiful are the feet of those who preach good news!" But they have not all heeded the gospel; for Isaiah says, "Lord, who has believed what he has heard from us?" So faith comes from what is heard, and what is heard comes by the preaching of Christ. (Romans 10:13-17)

Discipleship and mission go together: We need not wait to be perfect disciples before we share our faith with others. Of course, knowing about Jesus, Catholic doctrines, and how to evangelize most effectively will help us achieve our mission. Note that virtually all conversions in the New Testament stories we've mentioned impelled the converts to go tell others about Jesus right away. They took no training classes. Their passion flowed from their hearts. They could not help but talk about it. Lacking knowledge about doctrine or being a new disciple never should keep us from sharing Jesus. But to be mature in our faith, catechesis and formation are needed. Hopefully, as the converts in the New Testament stories grew in their faith, they also became better evangelists. To quote St. John Paul II:

> Within the whole process of evangelization, the aim of catechesis is to be the teaching and maturation stage, that is to say, the period in which the Christian, having

accepted by faith the person of Jesus Christ as the one Lord and having given Him complete adherence by sincere conversion of heart, endeavors to know better this Jesus to whom he has entrusted himself.[15]

Since conversion is our goal, we have to seek others' consent: Of course we want people to understand what is being asked of them when we discuss what it means to be Jesus' disciple. It is important that they know what it will cost. But our final goal is the other person's consent. Without it, there is no conversion. Therefore, we need to aim all of our work at getting someone to this point of decision. To quote St. John Paul II:

Many ... who have been baptized and been given a systematic catechesis and the sacraments still remain hesitant for a long time about committing their whole lives to Jesus Christ.[16]

Conversion is not one and done: It may sound surprising, but even if we have had a number of conversions, we have not finished turning to Jesus; we will need more. As a result, unless a person is about to die, being saved is not a onetime event. Instead, we give our all throughout life. Conversion is more a process than a moment for most. So, I encourage you to turn to Jesus again. Now. You may consider using this prayer:

Lord, I have let myself be deceived; in a thousand ways I have shunned your love, yet here I am once more, to renew my covenant with you. I need you. Save me once again, Lord, take me once more into your redeeming embrace.[17]

The goal of evangelization is helping others to have encounters with Jesus so they have the opportunity to choose to place Jesus at the center of their lives. This conversion is a radical reorientation, a repentance from sin, and a change of life, and it requires our consent.

Evangelization without personal repentance and conversion is incomplete. To be better evangelists, we must aim for the right thing!

ZACCHAEUS

was hated by his fellow Jews. As a tax collector, he collaborated with the Roman officials, who were enemies and oppressors of the Jews. On top of that, he cheated his fellow countrymen in order to make himself rich. Thus, he was an outcast living a lonely existence in the midst of a busy city. In his loneliness and sin, Zacchaeus wanted more out of life. He was seeking something and had heard stories about Jesus, the miracle-worker who ate with sinners and healed the outcasts. He must have hoped to encounter such a man.

Thus, when Jesus comes to town, Zacchaeus wants to see him. But, because he is too short, he cannot see over the vast crowd. So he risks doing what he knows will bring him ridicule—he climbs a tree like a child. Seeing him, Jesus calls out to him by name and asks to stay at his house. Zacchaeus receives Jesus and welcomes him into his home. Then he repents, promising to make restitution for all those he has cheated. Encounter. Invitation. Acceptance. Conversion. Repentance. Faith.

This is a story of a life changed. This is conversion.

QUESTIONS FOR CONSIDERATION

✳ *Is your evangelization aimed at consent?*
If not, how can you start to aim better?

✳ *Do you believe that grace works like magic?*
Why or why not?

✳ *In what way can you help others come to the point of conversion? What could you do better in order to facilitate conversion in the lives of those you want to evangelize?*

CHAPTER 6

THE STORY OF JESUS

I was eating lunch by myself in the cafeteria when a stunning young woman asked if she could sit with me. I immediately responded that she could. Looking around, I hoped that everyone in the vicinity noticed that I was the one sitting with the best-looking lady out of hundreds present. She asked me all the things that every college student asks—my name, where I was from, what my major was. We chatted for about sixty seconds before she said, "Do you know Jesus as your personal Lord and Savior?" I was rocked. I also got defensive. Who was she to ask me such a question? I quickly finished my lunch and politely excused myself a few minutes after we first met.

The problem was not with the question. The problem was the context of the question. If she had gotten to know me and if we built up trust and became friends before she asked me this question, it would not have been so threatening. Context matters, but the need to establish context should not keep us from eventually inviting people to grow with Jesus. If we believe that salvation is a good thing for everyone, then how could we not get around to eventually offering some Good News to others? In an earlier chapter, we talked about setting up the context for sharing the Good News by asking questions about the other person. In this chapter, we will discuss the heart of Good News. But first, I have some bad news. We are all sinners, and because of our sin, we deserve to be apart from God forever.

The good news is this is not the end of the story. Jesus has a remedy for this problem. God sent his Son, Jesus, to save us from sin and death. This is the Good News, or gospel. Catholics know the story, but we are not good at explicitly proclaiming it. That is something we can work on ourselves. But we have to start by understanding a certain word first. That word is *kerygma.*

Kerygma is not a word we hear every day. In modern Christian circles it is used rarely, so the word may not be familiar. If we have heard it, we must make sure we understand it correctly. Many answers to problems rest in a deeper understanding of what the *kerygma* is and how we should use it.

The word *kerygma* is Greek; it means "proclamation." To be precise, in the Christian context, the *kerygma* is a proclamation focused on Jesus' life, death, and resurrection. In short, Jesus took human nature to save us, and that is the primary message we deliver in our proclamations. We don't need to make it complicated or long. Make it a simple explanation that everyone can understand.

THE GOAL

Conversion is the goal of any proclamation of the *kerygma.* We need to be God's instruments so people may have an encounter with God, open themselves to his mercy and grace, and then become Jesus' disciples. That is the goal. We proclaim Jesus so we can make disciples for him. After conversion is accomplished, we can try to achieve other goals, such as catechesis. To quote the *General Directory of Catechesis*:

> Primary proclamation is addressed to non-believers and those living in religious indifference. Its functions are to proclaim the Gospel and to call to conversion. Catechesis, "distinct from the primary proclamation of the Gospel", promotes and matures initial conversion, educates the convert in the faith and incorporates him into the Christian community. The relationship between these two forms of the ministry of the word is, therefore, a relationship of complementary distinction. Primary proclamation, which every Christian is called to perform, is part of that "Go" which Jesus imposes on his disciples: it implies, therefore, a going-out, a haste, a message. Catechesis, however, starts with the condition indicated by Jesus himself: "whosoever believes", whosoever converts, whosoever decides.[18]

When we live with Jesus, our life is a series of moments that include these three elements:

1. Pre-evangelization: when we build relationships, earning the right to proclaim the *kerygma.*

2. Evangelization: clear proclamation of the *kerygma,* inviting a response, and the initial conversion of the person who is being evangelized.

3. Discipleship: following our Lord after conversion, including prayer, catechesis, service to people, and maturity in virtue.

This chapter's focus is on the content of the *kerygma.* We will first look at a number of different ways of delivering the good news about Jesus. While not complete ways, all are solid ways to present the *kerygma*. Remember, our aim is to keep our message simple. These possible ways of presenting the *kerygma* will be divided by the number of elements each one has or the theme of the story.

The Kerygma's Four Elements, Version A:

1. The plan that our loving God set in motion for humanity from the beginning of time includes a life with meaning, purpose, and relationship with God.

2. Adam and Even's original sin has separated humanity from God. We are not able to restore our relationship with God by our own power.

3. The life, death, and resurrection of God's Son, Jesus, are God's answers to our problem, enabling our salvation.

4. This grace calls all people to repent, believe in Jesus, and get baptized.

The Kerygma's Four Elements, Version B:

1. We were created by God to have a relationship with him. From the moment of Creation, God destined us to live with him forever.

2. We, through sin, broke the relationship with God we were supposed to have.

3. Jesus—fully God, fully human—came to us to heal that relationship by sacrificing his life, rising from the dead, and giving the Church to us so we could continue his saving mission.

4.   We can respond by electing to make Jesus our Lord, being baptized, repenting of our sins, and living in communion with him through his Church.[19]

The Kerygma Through Jesus' Kingdom in Four Parts:

1.   Jesus proclaims that the kingdom of God is present and meant for all to be a part of.

2.   Jesus is revealed as the King of all and invites us to be a part of his kingdom.

3.   Jesus' kingdom is at war with the devil's kingdom: Jesus will eventually defeat the devil, sin, and death.

4.   The Church builds up the kingdom: We are part of it, and we are called to holiness and mission.[20]

The *kerygma* can look a lot of ways in a narrative. Here is one way:

God created people to have a never-ending relationship with him. That's why he made us in his image and likeness. But people sinned, which broke the God-humanity relationship. Yet God planned to save us, sending Jesus, his Son, to come to us and win our souls for God. Jesus lived, died, and rose to conquer sin and death for all. He sacrificed his life so our lives can be eternal. Now that we have a chance to respond positively to this gift of grace and mercy, Jesus waits for us to consent, repent of our sins, believe in him, get baptized, and live a life that gives glory to God.

Then, when we die, we can live with him always. This is our choice. Do you want to choose this grace today?

Of course, there are better times than others to proclaim Good News. Just as the young woman in the cafeteria made an error by jumping into deep waters too quickly, we have to be able to discern how to best deliver such an important message. Here is some help for proclaiming the *kerygma*:

- Avoid church jargon when talking with those who do not have a relationship with Jesus. Insider language is fine for deep discussions about the finer points of Catholicism. But when you present the basic *kerygma*, you will not be talking about deep theology. Remember, a person does not need to know detailed theological arguments in order to love and believe in God.

- Before you begin, pray. Examine your own motives, be faithful, and be humble, and you have a chance to be a vessel of grace for people. You do not want to rely on your own power.

- Before you stop, be sure to invite a response. Catholics may think that is too Protestant, but it is not. Read Acts and note how often the apostles invited a response. They did so every time they preached. How you do it matters little. You can say an impromptu prayer, restate the baptismal promises, or recite the Creed prayerfully. Don't get caught up in the how—just make sure you help the other person make an act of faith.

- The moment may feel awkward, but that is fine.
  This is not easy, and it could be the most important
  event in the life of the person you are talking to.

Read Acts 2:14-42 to see St. Peter's great example of
proclaiming the story of Jesus and inviting a response. We
do not want our presentation of something so important
to be formulaic, though, so remember that this is just
one example. Avoid formulas and narrow methodologies.
There is no perfect way to evangelize in a world full of
unique people. Notice the many different ways Jesus
evangelized; he did not often repeat himself when
encountering someone new.

PETER

had denied Jesus, repented, and now waited for the promised Holy Spirit. I bet Pentecost was unlike anything he was expecting when it finally arrived. The apostles were filled with a spiritual fire that could not be contained, so they went into the streets and started to proclaim the *kerygma* to the people. Many thought they were drunk. But after they finished proclaiming the Good News, three thousand people were baptized. Three thousand souls born again!

Where is that kind of fruitfulness today? Why aren't our parishes places of conversion? Why aren't you and I more successful in our evangelization efforts? I suggest that we become more like St. Peter and the early Church—that we become much bolder in professing the gospel message and then inviting a response from others.

Maybe we need to respond to it ourselves, either for the first time or once again. Peter certainly was not without his flaws. He frequently stuck his foot in his mouth and made mistakes. Yet he was the first pope, the first leader of the Church after Jesus ascended to heaven. He was the first one to proclaim the gospel after Pentecost. He was the first apostle to raise someone from the dead. God powerfully used a sinful and limited man to change lives. We are all sinful and limited people, but if we allow him, God can change lives through you and me, too. We need to renew this apostolic preaching and not settle for anything less. In a few short generations following Pentecost, the world was changed—all because Peter decided to leave the Upper Room and obey the call to make disciples. Now it is our turn.

QUESTIONS FOR CONSIDERATION

✴ *Spend some time writing out the* kerygma *in your own words.*

✴ *Practice telling this story, without notes, to another disciple of Jesus. Ask for feedback.*

✴ *Who are some people in your life who need to hear and respond to the* kerygma? *Write down their names. How can you more boldly share the Good News with them and invite them to respond?*

CHAPTER 7

YOUR STORY MEETS JESUS' STORY

Stories can affect us in a big way. Remember a great film that moved you, such as *Schindler's List* or *Avengers: Endgame.* Call to mind the best book you have ever read and the way you felt after finishing it. Remember what you felt as you watched a news story of a soldier returning home from war and seeing his child for the first time.

Stories can move, inspire, teach—and they can change our minds. God can even use stories in our conversion. We need to hear stories, and we need to tell them. More than ever, we need to share our stories of how God has worked in us. To quote St. Paul VI, "Modern man listens more willingly to witnesses than to teachers, and if he does listen to teachers, it is because they are witnesses."[21]

Jesus told parables frequently. In fact, they comprise almost one-third of Jesus' teaching content in the four Gospels. His stories were often about everyday things. For example, Jesus talked about losing a coin and searching for it, calling for lost sheep, and baking bread. He used the stories to highlight truth or different aspects of a teaching he wanted others to connect with. Jesus was a gifted and powerful storyteller who knew how to draw others into the narrative he wanted to deliver.

WE ARE MADE FOR STORIES

Think of the last few presidential elections. What catchphrases sum up each winning candidacy? For President Obama's campaign, it was "hope and change." President Trump's campaign used "make America great again." These phrases are part of larger stories that highlight the different views each candidate was promising. Obama and Trump told competing stories that appealed to vastly different audiences, and yet each story led to victory on election day. Stories can change the history of the world.

Now think of the stories that are part of your life. If you have had an encounter with Jesus that began a conversion to become his disciple, you have a story, a testimony. In a testimony, a person tells how God has changed his or her life. Role models for testimony can be St. Paul, St. Peter, and St. John, who shared their conversion stories in Scripture. So did early Christians. They knew how powerful stories can be. In the Acts of the Apostles, Luke recounts several different people's testimonies. These stories tell how each person met Jesus, and sharing the story was something they did naturally. When you share your own testimony, do so naturally and narratively.

Perhaps you believe that nobody would want to hear your story because it is not dramatic enough. Choosing Jesus means you have a story, even if it is not dramatic. One of our most memorable saints, Thérèse of Lisieux, had a somewhat idyllic life, raised by two saints and encountering Jesus often. She may never have committed a mortal sin, never been without the state of grace after her baptism. Her story of her many encounters with Jesus was not dramatic, but it has impacted millions. Your story is yours. It might be like St. Paul's experience of being struck down, or it might be seemingly ho-hum. It doesn't matter. Tell it, and God can use it to influence people.

If you don't have a story, I invite you to put Jesus at the center of your life now. Do not delay the day of salvation.

PERSONAL STORIES DO WHAT OBJECTIVE FACTS CANNOT

We can never assume that others will agree with us simply because we speak the truth. Personal testimony, however, can reach many hearts. Your witness about God working in you and changing your life can do many things:

- It gives evidence that is uniquely yours. Your story is real. It illustrates that your faith is genuine and that God is active in you.

- It can raise important topics for others and for yourself. It can trigger questions in others.

- Personal stories are hard to argue with. Others might not believe that what happened for you could happen for them, but they will rarely tell you that your encounter with God was false.

- It illustrates the power of God in a powerful, personal way. It can also show how God offers grace.

- It does not threaten others. Because it is a story from your life, it is rarely seen as a threat.

The witness of your life and the narrative you offer to others can be considered subjective good news, a subjective gospel message. God's grace has been poured into your soul, and you are his disciple. That is good news! Just as the objective *kerygma* is important, so is your subjective story.

But always remember that behind every discussion, debate, and dialogue are human beings whom God loves more than anything else. Your job is to connect them with this love, not prove them wrong. Since our modern culture values storytelling over truth-telling, we have to orient truth to be told more through narratives than propositions.

Furthermore, these objective and subjective gospels can link up to comprise a single message. It is possible to blend your story with the story of Jesus in one unique narrative. This skill, a wonderful talent, is shown by Paul in Acts 22:1-21, Acts 26, and Philippians 3:4-17.

SHARING YOUR TESTIMONY

If you want to be able to share your witness with people effectively, here are some ideas:

- Give examples of changes in your life that God's presence has caused. If your life has not changed, consider how God may be calling you to change it.

- Give examples of times you have felt the presence of God with his forgiveness, grace, mercy, or love.

- If you have ever had a moment in prayer that was deep, talk about it.

- Describe ways in which God has helped you.

- If God has comforted you or made you feel at peace or fulfilled, give examples.

Now think about these three basic elements:

Your Life Before You Knew Jesus

Start with some background information. Give examples of life issues and how you dealt with them before you had an encounter with Jesus that led to your conversion. Your life probably had good times as well as bad. You will want to be able to share some good things, not just the negative. But you will also want to note things that were missing or out of sorts without Jesus as your leader. When telling your background story, give concrete examples but not too many details—leave out details that are important to you but not to those listening to your story. Also avoid sharing too much detail about your past sins. There is no reason to go into detail about what you did or why you did it. You may scandalize others or yourself in doing so.

While talking about mistakes, sins, or problems in your past, avoid judging your life harshly. That might discourage those who are in a similar place. If you tell others that you were an idiot for committing a certain sin that they are currently committing, they may just shut down and not listen any longer. They may feel that you think they are also idiots.

Finally, relate to your audience. Do not use religious words unless you define them.

When You Encountered Jesus – Your Conversion

This is the key part of your story, so clearly state *when* you encountered Jesus, *how* you encountered Jesus, and *what* happened when you encountered Jesus. Concentrate your story on when you encountered him, on when you made your decision to follow him, and on your conversion. Describe how you felt, what you did or said, and how you reacted. If your conversion happened over days, months, or years, talk about how things changed and talk about the big moments.

Talk about Jesus personally and use his name frequently in your narrative. Be careful not to fall into a preaching or teaching mode. While preaching may be important at some point, you want to be a storyteller when sharing your conversion.

Life After Your Conversion

When talking about the difference that Jesus has made in your life, state clearly what has changed. Give examples. What is no longer part of your life? Talk about what you have received. State things you now do differently. You do not want to make your present life seem like an unattainable fantasy, so be real about your struggles. At the same time, share your hope and the way knowing Jesus is transforming you.

Your ending can be a simple invitation. You can simply say that Jesus wants to be a part of every person's life or something similar.

The following is an example of how I share my story that illustrates the three basic elements.

MY STORY

I was raised in a very Catholic family. So Catholic that my father was named "Catholic Youth of the Nation" while in college. My mother is a prayer warrior. Both are very devout and good disciples. Nonetheless, I decided I didn't want to be a Catholic myself and stopped going to Mass while in college.

I did all the things you think of when you think of a wild college lifestyle. I thought happiness was at the bottom of a beer bottle and in relationships with women. Still, I couldn't kick the feeling that life really was about something more. I felt guilty for how I treated others, and deep down I wanted more from my life, but I didn't know how to attain it. It was at this time that I was blessed to meet some young men who invited me to go on a church retreat. I went only because of the promise that beautiful young women were going too. Little did I know what God had in store for me.

While on the retreat, I heard the gospel proclaimed and then had an opportunity to go to confession. At this point, I was divided. Part of me really wanted to go and the other part really didn't. I battled for almost thirty minutes internally before deciding to give it a try. It was the best thing that ever happened to me. I started with all the sins I was most ashamed of. When I was done, I was surprised the priest didn't scold me. Instead he looked at me and said, "There is nothing you can do to make God stop loving you." I was rocked. For the first time in my life, I knew God loved me right in my sinful mess. I knew God forgave my sins, and I walked out free and at peace.

I knelt down and prayed the most sincere prayer of my life. I told Jesus that I wanted to give my life to him and follow him. I was a different man walking out of that confessional than I was walking in. I felt unburdened and free from guilt. I was alive in Jesus and so joyful, I couldn't contain it.

After the retreat, I was drawn into a community of more mature disciples who helped show me what the life of a follower of Jesus was all about. I started to pray. I started to work on my sinful habits. I was challenged to grow. Of course, I didn't do it perfectly and still don't, but I know God loves me right in the midst of my imperfections, just like he loves you. We don't need to be perfect before we ask Jesus to be a part of our lives; we just need to be open.

SAUL was an accessory to murder. In fact, he helped murder the first Christian martyr, Stephen. But God wanted to use him for a powerful purpose: to spread the gospel. Saul had an encounter with Jesus while traveling to arrest Christian disciples. After this, Saul started to go by the name Paul because he was a different man. His encounter led to a conversion, and this conversion became part of his testimony that he would share with others.

St. Paul is the author of more books of the Bible than anyone else. His teachings have had a deep impact on Christianity and the world. God used this sinful man's story to bring about untold numbers of conversions. He was a sinner who opened his life up to grace, told the story of how Jesus changed his life, proclaimed the gospel, and then invited others to become disciples of Jesus, as well. This is the formula for us, too. Are you the next great evangelist the world needs? You won't know until you say yes to Jesus.

QUESTIONS FOR CONSIDERATION

✴ *Be specific in describing your life before your encounter with Jesus.*

✴ *Describe how you encountered Jesus. What happened?*

✴ *Write out how your life is now different.*
What has changed?

✳ *Practice sharing your testimony with another disciple.*

✳ *Ask God to give you an opportunity to share your testimony with someone else. When you find this opportunity, share your testimony boldly.*

CHAPTER 8

PRAYER AND THE POWER OF INTERCESSION

In 1592 Pope Clement VIII had many concerns to deal with. There were disagreements about theology that divided religious orders, scandals involving Church leaders, invasions from other countries, and civil wars. One particular concern was the thirty-year religious war in France. King Henry IV, a Calvinist, was leading one side of the war, and Clement sought to end the war, convert Henry to Catholicism, and heal the wounds the conflict caused. Clement's way of dealing with the problem was to institute a period of prayer before the Blessed Sacrament.[22] The results were quite remarkable.

Clement was able to convert Henry IV. Once he was convinced that Henry's conversion was authentic (and not just for political reasons), the war came to an end and the king was received into the Catholic Church. Eventually peace was established between France and Spain, thus ending many long years of war and tension.

Many saints began to arise from the areas where the time of prayer was centered. One of these saints was St. Francis de Sales. The year after Clement began the period of prayer for France, Francis was ordained a priest and began to evangelize the area around Geneva, a hotbed of Calvinism. In this area most of the people had left the Catholic Church and become Calvinists. Yet St. Francis de Sales was credited with bringing these tens of thousands of people back to the Catholic Church in just a few years! Because of his fruitfulness, he was appointed bishop of Geneva.[23]

But the story does not end there. This revival in France led to renewing the local churches, which then formed missionary disciples who sent out missionaries. These missionaries eventually took the Catholic Faith to other parts of the world, including Louisiana, Canada, Vietnam, and Madagascar.

A renewal that is born of prayer is not unusual. In fact, every age of Church renewal has been born out of intense and prolonged prayer.

GOD WORKING THROUGH US

If we are to be potential agents of conversion in other people's lives, we ourselves must be transformed first. We must turn our lives over to God daily and open our hearts to his grace. Our personal prayer is the foundation. Our personal prayer life is indispensable and irreplaceable. Our evangelization efforts will not have God's power otherwise. In fact, efforts to evangelize will be in vain if we are not praying. Pope Benedict XVI said, "Apostolic and missionary fruitfulness is not principally due to programmes and pastoral methods that are cleverly drawn up and 'efficient', but is the result of the community's constant prayer."[24]

The fruits of prayer are many, but I would like to highlight several. First of all, when we have a relationship with God, forged through prayer, we start to attain the vision of God for our lives. A desire for holiness wells up, and we want to grow ever closer to God. The more our wills align with the will of God, the more joy we gain for the mission God has for us. Our evangelization becomes easier and more joy-filled, even if the work remains hard.

Furthermore, we start to long for and love the salvation of others more and more. Like God, we greatly desire the salvation of all people. This growing longing for the salvation of others means that we cannot help sharing the gospel, and our evangelization efforts are multiplied through our prayer.

Finally, as we are better able to discern the best ways to evangelize others, we start to see our evangelization becoming more fruitful. Thus, our passion and energy grow because we see more and more fruit coming from our efforts.

Imagine how St. Francis de Sales felt when he began his mission. Sent to a largely fallen-away population of people who rejected Catholicism, he must have worried that he would not be up to the task. He was rejected and despised. Still he persisted in his mission. The strength to continue was found in a faithfulness born out of prayer. When he started to see conversion and change in people, this must have enlivened him to continue to pray and evangelize more. Thus, the two went hand in hand: evangelical fruitfulness and prayer uniting to change thousands of lives.

If we want to share this kind of fruitfulness, we too must pray fervently.

WE ARE NOT ALONE

While our personal prayer is powerful and necessary, it is not the only way we ought to pray. We also ought to pray with those around us. Communal prayer takes place in the Eucharist and by partaking in the other sacraments. The Eucharist is the heart of our mission. It is what gives us strength for our mission, and one of our primary goals should be bringing others to the Eucharist.

During Mass we also pray for the world when we unite our intercession together in the Prayer of the Faithful. Other forms of communal prayer include Holy Hours, perpetual Adoration of the Blessed Sacrament, praying the Rosary as a community, and prayer groups.

Communal prayer is an invitation for the Holy Spirit to change the spiritual climate of a community. When this happens, the local parish community becomes a vehicle of grace for others, and the growing spiritual openness leads to more conversions. Prayer opens the door for God to do the hard work in hearts and frees us from feeling responsible for this.

PRAYER TEAMS FOR LOCAL EVANGELIZATION EFFORTS

If a local group of Catholics wants to be fruitful, I highly recommend forming an intercessory prayer team. When I started my apostolate, Catholic Missionary Disciples, I asked a group of faithful Catholic prayer warriors to pray for its success. I can clearly see the fruit of their prayers because the ways in which God has pushed us forward are not the ways I thought things could go. God had much better plans!

If a group of evangelists is parish based, getting together in person to pray is best. The group can meet to share and pray for intentions. A bit of awkwardness about praying together is to be expected, but all should still be encouraged to pray out loud. The point is not to dwell only on needs or negative things to overcome. Rather, it should be a combination of several forms of prayer. Praise and worship God for who he is. Thank God for his blessings. Adore God for his sake.

The group might choose to have a time of adoration together, pray the Rosary, do prayer walks around parish neighborhoods, or meditate on Sacred Scripture using *lectio divina*. A powerful way to break through any strong barriers is to fast for particular petitions. Pray for specific people, works of evangelization, and efforts of discipleship. These particular intentions need to be expressed every time the group gets together. Make sure there is time for feedback, for sharing how the prayers are being answered.

Whoever is leading the group should regularly ask the leadership of the parish, especially the pastor, for prayer intentions and then provide feedback.

I recommend keeping a written list of petitions; the group should continue to discern the needs on the list in an ongoing manner. If any supernatural signs and wonders occur, discuss what happened and give thanks and praise to God. If prayers are answered, share with the group and thank God.

Intercession requires surrender—we will not always see or hear about the fruit of our prayers. Don't forget to invite the saints and angels to pray with us and for us. They pray better than we do! Marian prayer should be part of our devotion, too, because that means we are learning from the first disciple of Jesus, his mother.

The purpose of a prayer team includes building unity, sharing a vision, discerning God's will, breaking through strongholds of the enemy, inviting the Holy Spirit to lead our efforts, allowing God to teach us how to pray, growing as missionary disciples, and not relying on our own power and effort. Pope Francis wrote, "Let us call upon him today, firmly rooted in prayer, for without prayer all our activity risks being fruitless and our message empty. Jesus wants evangelizers who proclaim the good news not only with words, but above all by a life transfigured by God's presence."[25]

When we start to discern who might be a good member of our prayer team, look for disciples who have a personal prayer life. The people who have charisms of intercessory prayer, discernment of spirits, prophecy, music, encouragement, and leadership might also be good candidates. If someone asks to be a member, let him or her try it out on a trial basis. Look for those who are consistent in their commitments and have a heart for serving others. Also, make sure they know the cost of spiritual warfare they are taking on. Intercession is about discipline more than desire.

ST. THÉRÈSE – OUR MODEL

St. Thérèse is the patroness of missionaries, though she never left the convent as an adult. While her heart desired to be fruitful, God wanted to use her prayers for the fruitfulness of other members of the Church. Thus, she lived in the cloister, praying for the universal Church, and her powerful prayers have been the source of countless conversions.

Her deep love for the salvation of the world drove her deeper into intimacy with Jesus, the one who saves. This is why she could say that her vocation was love, and this vocation was lived out in and through her prayer. St. Thérèse could not keep Jesus to herself—her love for him spilled out to others. We, too, can be fruitful disciples, if only we pray.

MARY is a powerful intercessor for others. We can

learn how to intercede from her example. Before Jesus was ready to start his active ministry, he went to a wedding feast at Cana. Weddings in the time of Jesus lasted for several days. Thus, a lot of food and drink was necessary to celebrate the union of husband and wife. At this wedding the newlyweds run out of wine. Can you imagine how devastating this could be to the celebration?

But Mary intercedes on their behalf. When she tells Jesus about the problem, his reaction is somewhat surprising. Instead of immediately doing as she requests, he asks how this is his concern. Mary does not answer the question; instead she turns and asks the servants to do what Jesus tells them to do.

I imagine Mary being like many strong mothers who expect to be listened to the first time and not repeat themselves because they trust that their children will do what they ask. Mary's faith in Jesus is not misplaced—he changes many gallons of water into wine, and the feast continues even better than before.

We, too, need to have the faith of Mary. We need to trust that Jesus cares, will act, and will do what is best for others. This starts and ends with fervent prayers and with asking Mary to intercede also on our behalf.

QUESTIONS FOR CONSIDERATION

✳ *Who should you be praying for? Write their names now.*

✳ *How can your parish or prayer team pray for particular groups of fallen-away Catholics in your community?*

✳ *If you are working in a group and do not have an intercessory prayer team, map out the steps to establishing one and calendar when you will get them done.*

CHAPTER 9

EVANGELIZING
AT HOME

For many Catholics, their family is the hardest group to evangelize. But if there is one group we are called to evangelize, it is our family. The real question is how we can best do it. We have to accept that often there are no easy answers, and things can get quite messy. In fact, it is best if we embrace the mess up front.

I know elderly parents who have been praying for their children's conversions for decades. This is always the first step—never give up. Never stop praying. Never stop hoping. Trust that the power and sovereignty of God will work through us. Prayer is the means by which we allow God to do miraculous things we cannot do alone.

Next, understand that evangelization is not about having one conversation and throwing everything we have into it. That is like giving our kids one talk about sexuality and thinking it is enough. (It isn't!) We have to think long term. Evangelization is not just a task that we check off a list so we can get back to the real things in life. Rather, evangelization is a lifestyle born out of understanding our very reason for existing. If we believe that God made us—everyone—for heaven, then we cannot just do our evangelical work once in a while. Rather, it should naturally flow out of our lives, habits, and conversations.

BREAK THE SILENCE

In many parts of the Church, we have a code of silence. This silence means that Jesus is rarely talked about explicitly. The result is that many people think they know who Jesus is when they really do not. Our job is to discern when it is appropriate to break this code of silence because without hearing about Jesus, nobody can follow him. We have to talk about our relationship with Jesus, especially with our family.

Most people want to have meaningful discussions. The problems arise when we get into contentious disagreements and arguments. Family history can heighten these issues, especially when there is a history of dysfunction. Rarely do others have their hearts transformed in the heat of an argument. The aim of evangelization is not to prove someone wrong. As Fulton Sheen supposedly quipped, "Win an argument, lose a soul." Our job is not to prove a point, win an argument, come out on top of a debate, or conquer another's view. Rather, it is to help someone grow closer to Jesus.

How we talk about God needs to be discerned. We can share stories about our lives, apply Catholic principles to tough situations, or just allow God to lead us. Whatever we do, do not avoid faith or religion. Even if it can be uncomfortable, our demeanor and attitude will set the tone more than the topic. By smiling, being kind, and loving the other person, we can break the silence and possibly help our family members grow closer to God.

TREAT THEM AS YOU WANT TO BE TREATED

Yes, we have a history with our family. But unless we treat them with respect and kindness, they will not respond with respect or kindness. In my own family, many nonbelievers avoid talking about anything religious because they are afraid I am going to "try to change their minds."

Part of this is due to my immaturity as a Christian along with a zealousness that was too in-your-face. I probably drove them further away from God due to my approach. I was an insufficient evangelist for the task at hand, and while I am still insufficient, the good news is that God is not. He has helped me to continue to grow and mature as a Catholic. While I am better, I am not perfect. While I am kinder, I am not kind enough. When it comes to family relationships, there is a lot of work to do. Yet some of my relationships are better than they have ever been because I have invested many years in loving my family better than I have in the past.

I have four siblings, with one younger than I am. When we were kids, we rarely got along, and I was a mean big brother. I pushed my little sister away. When I had a conversion, my rough personality still kept my sister at arm's length. At one point I realized how bad I was as a brother, and I apologized and asked for forgiveness. This helped set us on a new course, and our relationship has never been better. So apologize if you have to—it's good for your soul and your relationships.

Our words will mean little if our lives do not reflect the words we proclaim. So another step in treating our families well is to become better people ourselves. Never stop growing and maturing as a Christian. A transformed life is a great way to witness to the power of God working through us.

Ultimately, we will have to get to the basics. This is done by talking about our own relationship with Jesus (see chapter 7) and proclaiming the *kerygma* (see chapter 6). These are the two most important stories we can tell: how God has changed our lives and how God has changed the world.

When I teach others to evangelize, the most common questions I get revolve around how best to evangelize family members who have left the Catholic Church. You likely are familiar with the statistics about fallen-away Catholics who no longer attend Mass or practice the Faith. Behind those numbers are people and families. Every fallen-away Catholic has a family. Each has a soul and a destiny. All Catholics, nonpracticing ones included, need Jesus. The fallen-away may not know they need Jesus, but they still have a right to evangelization that is the best we can give. We owe each person that much.

There is true heartbreak for a parent when a child walks away from the Catholic Church. The pain and anguish cut deep. You cannot know how sad these situations are unless you have tried to comfort and encourage many dads and moms whose adult children live far from God. These Catholic parents' biggest regret is that they did not do enough to evangelize their kids. They regret that they did not do enough to teach their children to be disciples. Is there anything we can do to keep our children in the Church? Try these measures if your children are still at home.

INTENTIONAL PARENTING

While using an app to track my fourteen-year-old daughter's texts, I saw a message from her in which she told a friend she wasn't doing much, "just finished talking to Jesus." Talk about being a proud dad! My daughter could have been doing anything, but she chose to spend her time reading the Bible and praying. This is our goal as parents. We want our children to have a personal relationship with Jesus. That relationship is rooted in prayer and leads to a life-giving Faith, responsible choices, and personal and spiritual maturity.

Getting there is the challenge. Even kids from holy Catholic families may elect to stray from the Church.

I know scores of Catholic parents who teach their kids prayers, pray with their kids, make time for family prayer, and let their kids catch them praying regularly. That is all indispensable, but most families are missing a key ingredient: parents do not expect that their children will make time for daily prayer on their own. This is key. Our own family has stressed the importance of prayer time in many ways. When the kids were very young, we had it on a to-do list. As they got older, we started shifting the responsibility to them, asking them daily if they had made time for Jesus. We built a culture of personal prayer into our family, and it shows—all five of our kids spend time by themselves in prayer.

We built a culture at home emphasizing that God only has children, no grandkids. That helps our children know that no one can depend on parents or anyone else to get us into heaven. Each person has to place his or her own faith in Jesus for salvation. There is no other way once we are old enough to make decisions freely. These kinds of faith discussions can happen frequently if we set the topic and tone in our households.

NURTURE THE FAITH

Have you ever walked on a college campus and noticed the shortcuts that people have made through the grass? Nothing keeps that from taking place. "Keep off" signs, fences, slogans—nothing works. The students will make their own paths.

Parenting is like this, too. Children, like adults, will want to take the easy way. They seek shortcuts, wanting comfort and simplicity. They want to be catered to. We adults have the same tendency, so we can't expect children to be different.

While campus groundskeepers can't force students to keep off the grass, they can build paths through the grass. If change is inevitable, don't fight it. Guide it. In our current culture, change is inevitable. Kids grow, mature, and change constantly. Our job as parents is to direct the change.

For example, my wife and I know we cannot keep screens out of the lives of our children. So we do our best to direct them in age-appropriate ways. Each child gets a phone around age twelve. It is for texting and talking and is only used at certain times and for specific lengths of time. At sixteen, they can use data, but we use strict filtering and enforce rules. Our goal is to ensure that, when they leave home, they are not addicted to the phone or have unhealthy phone habits, like viewing porn.

All kids grow up. Directing that growth is up to the parents. Our goal as parents should be helping our children become responsible adults who can make wise decisions on their own. How do you make an immature Catholic kid into a mature Catholic disciple? A good way is to give children as many chances as possible to experience conversion, whether the first conversion to follow Jesus or a conversion that deepens that choice.

My wife and I have invested much time, money, and effort to place our children into just such situations. First, we enrolled the children in a school with a positive Christian culture. It is not perfect, but the school presents the Faith as acceptable and attractive. That is not common in schools, even Catholic schools. We provided our kids with other opportunities, such as Bible-study groups, youth groups in the parish, camps for Catholics, and youth conferences. We have set up as many opportunities as we can.

We also make space for conversion by offering the kids the opportunity to choose to forgive, grant mercy, show virtue, and accept grace. When they have a hard time, we encourage them to pray. If they mess up, we take them to confession. If they feel apart from God, we ask them to invite their Creator to take part in the situation. We have taught them to pray, repent, and choose virtue.

As a result of our efforts, our children are given as many opportunities as we can give them to encounter Jesus, making conversion a natural element in our family.

WRESTLING WITH TRUTH

A few years back, one of our children told me a friend—a girl—was attracted to girls and was dating a female. My kid did not know how to respond to this and was having a tough time loving that friend while also recognizing the Church's teaching that sexual behavior outside of marriage is always wrong. We talked about this a lot, but the internal struggle continued. I provided answers, but more importantly, I tried helping my child process the matter. Boiled down, our chats went something like this:

Me – *How does this situation make you feel?*

Kid – *I'm confused. My feelings are all mixed up.*

Me – *Do you still love your friend and want the best for her?*

Kid – *Sure! I also know God loves her, and he wants her to make better choices about her sexual relationships.*

Me – *Are those decisions yours to make for her?*

Kid – *No.*

Me – *With all this tension you feel, how can you love her in this moment?*

Kid – *I don't know.*

Me – *What would be more loving: end the friendship or stay her friend.*

Kid – *Be her friend.*

Me – *I think you're right. But how will that look?*

Kid – *Huh?*

Me – *How can you still love her while also not approving of all her choices or making those choices for her?*

Kid – *I can accept her, know God loves her, and spend time with her, but not validate that all her decisions are correct or good.*

Me – *I think you are on the right track. Let's bring God in. Want to pray about this?*

A key to guiding and mentoring instead of forcing is to ask open-ended questions that lead others to think through matters. Our questions should also be a guide to help our children reach the most prudent and holy decisions. Our children will struggle with certain parts of following Jesus and the Church. That happens to everyone. So give kids room to ask questions, including tough questions. We can ask tough ones, too. We want kids to have space to wrestle, and we want them to have something to anchor themselves to. The truths of Jesus and his Church give us just that. Accepting these truths makes the Faith personal, but it doesn't happen all at once. Be sure to balance teaching with space to ask questions, while always challenging the kids never to settle for the easy or convenient solution.

Today, young Christians often fail to analyze the harmful aspects of culture. Instead, they soak them in. They accept the entire culture as worthwhile—even valuable—and then they hear their Faith tell them something different. In response, the Church is reactive. We don't form kids into disciples of Jesus first and then send them into the world. Instead, we allow the world to shape them, and we react. Who has the upper hand? The world and the culture. That is why we must be proactive: we must form the hearts, minds, consciences, and souls of our children instead of allowing the world to tell them how to be happy. I cannot emphasize this enough.

Reactive parenting will most likely fail our children. Someone or something will fill the formation void. That goes for tough topics like sexuality, relationships, sin, and pride. If we are not involved as parents to guide, teach, talk, and love, we risk being brushed aside in favor of other influences.

We may fall into the trap of "engaging" our kids (teens especially) rather than challenging them to live the tenets of their Faith. Engaging and challenging are not necessarily mutually exclusive. If we do both successfully, they won't be contradictory. But today, parents seem to want to entertain teenagers first and foremost. Too frequently, parents leave the faith formation to the churches and schools. They don't model or teach the Faith at home. Make the Church relevant, but not at the expense of the call to be holy and to follow the gospel.

FOOD!

We try to eat dinner together as a family every day. During the meal we discuss feelings, friends, cultural matters, and so on. Sometimes we talk about Dad's grumpiness or how one sibling is annoying another. We also talk about the content of the Faith by using great teaching tools, including the Theology of the Body, family prayers, the Church's Sunday readings, and a lot more.

For many young people, a huge obstacle to faith is the Church's teaching on sexuality. That should be no surprise because of the Church's opposition to the modern concept of sex. If we do not have anything to say yes to about sexuality, then the Church's teaching about sexuality sounds like just a big NO. But that is not the case. When we say no to premarital sex, contraception, abortion, and other sins surrounding sexuality, that means we affirm a big YES to God, life, purity, chastity, healthy and whole relationships, integrity, and more. But if all a kid hears is NO, then the other teachings don't make sense. The solution? Age-appropriate teaching from parents about sexuality, backed up by the teaching found in the Theology of the Body.

These strategies and techniques are not foolproof. Every kid still has free will, the gift that we love in ourselves and hate in everyone else. So, never pass up a teachable moment, a moment to pray, or a moment to invest in our kids. It is the way we can feed a good relationship with Mom and Dad that can pay off in the end.

WHAT JESUS WANTS

Remember, Jesus wants our children to reach heaven more than we do. We can never wait for other people to evangelize our kids. That is our job. That is the purpose of Jesus' Church: making disciples of all people. But each family—the domestic Church—is irreplaceable! Most parishes are struggling to survive, so we cannot wait for the parish or any other servant of the Church to do our evangelizing for us. We hope they can support us, but that support sometimes comes up short.

Our top goal as parents is getting our children to heaven. This must be our unwavering vision. To achieve that goal, we have to spend time with our kids. If we don't, we won't have a deep impact on them. Quality time can never be a replacement for the quantity of time we are around our families. The less time we are around our kids, the fewer opportunities we have to make an impact on them. Think of this as the family's "ordinary time." While most of the year is full of it, without this time we are going to struggle to raise disciples.

When our kids are grown and leave home, we may be able to be their friends. Until then, we must be the parents they need us to be. We must establish boundaries and live by them. It is crucial that we love our kids. Hug them and tell them we love them. Be involved in what they do. Don't smother, but be present. Never settle for being their pal. Be especially vigilant with modern technology.

Finally, we must pray for our kids. Do it every day.

IN JOHN 4:46-54, St. John recounts a remarkable story.

There is a government official who begs Jesus to heal his son, who is near death. This man is from Capernaum, and yet he goes to Jesus in Cana, about twenty miles away. Jesus challenges the man's faith and tells him that he will not believe, yet the man persists and asks Jesus to go to his son and heal him. Jesus responds that the man can leave because Jesus will indeed do what he asks. The man leaves because he believes.

When he arrives home, his son is healed. He asks his servants when the healing happened, and they tell him that it was at the same time that Jesus promised to heal his son. Then the most remarkable thing happens. The man and his entire house come to believe in Jesus. Notice that this is not just one person, but the entire house. Wife. Children. Servants. They all believe.

While our first priority is to get ourselves into heaven, we need to make sure we do everything we can to get our family there, too, just as this official did. We want all of our household to believe in Jesus.

QUESTIONS FOR CONSIDERATION

✳ *Name some family whom you believe you may be called to evangelize.*

✳ *What are some of the ways that you might share your faith with them?*

✳ *What is your internal reaction when you think about evangelizing them?*

✳ *What barriers may block your ability to evangelize them?*

✳ *How are you intentionally helping your children grow in faith?*

✳ *What family habits might you need to establish with your children?*

CHAPTER 10

EVANGELIZING AT WORK

As a young adult, all the people I worked with were older than I was, and none of them were Christians. I knew I was called to evangelize them, but I felt unequipped, afraid, and alone. In addition, many of them were openly hostile to the Catholic Church. I had a big hill to climb—but I did it anyway.

Two of the most common questions people ask Catholic leaders are "How can I evangelize my family?" and "How can I evangelize at work?" We talked about family in the last chapter. In this chapter, I will address the important question of evangelizing at work.

CAUTION: WORKERS AHEAD

If the Catholic Church is going to "make disciples of all nations," then we must go to the world and do our best to evangelize those who are far from God. In the workplace, many Catholics interact mostly with non-Catholics or non-Christians who have little or no faith. To evangelize the world, we have to get better at evangelizing at work.

There are multiple barriers to being an effective workplace evangelist. There are corporate politics and personality dynamics. Cultural barriers exist, including the unwritten rule that we are not supposed to talk about things at work that are too personal. In our modern climate, it is easy to be labeled as intolerant or bigoted. Finally, there are the fears that evangelizing within the workplace could harm our careers or even cost us our jobs. These fears are real, and we should not minimize them.

Evangelizing others has always required boldness and courage. But being bold does not mean being overbearing, in-your-face, or pushy. In fact, if we act that way, our chances of reaching people are slim to none. So how do we share our faith courageously yet with prudence and tact?

Well, first, do not overthink things. Next, remember that evangelization is not a formula to be presented but an opportunity to be a witness of Jesus' love for the world. Evangelization needs to be thought of less as something we do and more as a result of who we are. That is why it is important to start by living out our faith as authentically as we can.

BE A GOOD EMPLOYEE

The first step to evangelizing others is to be good at our jobs. Work hard. Grow in our craft. Be humble. Learn. Serve. Excel. Follow the rules. Be exceptionally ethical in our work. This kind of excellence in the workplace will help us stand out and be admired. By itself, it is the first step to showing that we do things differently than many others who are there merely to get a paycheck.

While being an excellent employee is a nice start, we cannot stop there. We also need to practice our faith at work. We need to make sure we are applying the high moral standards of the Catholic Church to how we work. Do not participate in workplace gossip. Treat others with kindness. Be fair and just to our clients as well as our employer. Forgive others who treat us badly. Be a peacemaker between coworkers who do not like one another. This kind of witness of life carries great weight with the world that thinks Catholics are just judgmental bigots. Furthermore, if we do not live out our faith at work, we can easily be dismissed as hypocrites and people who do not walk the walk. Lazy, incompetent, and poor employees will never make good evangelists at work.

CRACK OPEN THE DOOR

When I realized I was called to actively witness to my faith, I started by merely letting others know that my faith was something important to me. If it was a Monday and someone asked me what I did the past weekend, I would make sure that part of my answer included that we went to Mass and had a restful Sunday enjoying our time together as a family. This was delivered in a matter-of-fact way. I would allow that to open the door for further conversation. I was not obnoxious about the way I talked about my faith, but I made sure I put it all on the table.

We cannot expect others to ask us about our faith. Waiting for others to take the initiative is a fatal flaw of workplace evangelization. We must give ourselves permission to take a small risk and start a conversation about God. Without taking the initiative ourselves, we will most likely have few meaningful conversations.

Once others knew I was Catholic, I would look for opportunities to allow them to ask me questions. One man showed mild interest in Catholicism, so I listened actively to his questions and told him to let me know if he ever had more questions. About a month later, he did ask me some questions, and we had a wonderful conversation about God, faith, and Catholicism. This was merely a natural outgrowth of our growing relationship.

BE A GOOD FRIEND

People trust friends, not just coworkers. If we want to be able to truly evangelize others, then our relationships must extend beyond the workplace. Ask someone to lunch. Invite a coworker to dinner with the family. Go get a beer with others after work. In a culture where people feel more and more disconnected and yet still have a deep desire for meaningful relationships, Catholics can help fill that void. How else are the lost going to be found if we are not actively seeking them out?

Something that almost always works is to get beyond the small talk and the shallow conversations that often infect a place of work. Most people want to talk about things that matter, but either they are waiting for someone else to take the initiative or they do not know how to have such conversations at work. We can talk about our own families. Mention our desires and dreams for the future. Open up about a fear we have (but do not get too deep too fast). Lead with a bit of vulnerability. Whatever it is, steer the conversation to something meaningful, then listen actively to what they say.

This is a good time to remind ourselves that understanding another person's viewpoint does not mean we have to agree with him or her. Through this kind of ongoing friendship, we show that we care about the other person as a person, not just a coworker or a project. Those who work with us will not always listen if we are merely coworkers, but they are much more likely to do so if we are friends.

INVITE CATHOLIC FRIENDS TO HELP

Postmodern people value authenticity in relationships. Having authentic Catholic friends who can help us witness to our coworkers is invaluable. Imagine having a birthday party and inviting friends from work and church. They have fun together, and your coworkers start to realize that you are the same person at home, church, and work. Your life is integrated. You truly are someone who lives an authentic Christian lifestyle, and following Jesus really does inform every aspect of your life.

This is the kind of witness that a community of disciples can provide. After we build a strong enough friendship with our coworkers, we earn the right to go to the next step. That could be an invitation to a Bible study. It could be sharing our conversion stories. It may even mean proclaiming the Good News and inviting a response of faith and repentance.

PRAY FOR OTHERS

If we would be effective workplace evangelists, God will be the one acting through us. Our own effort and strategy is meaningless if the Holy Spirit is not the one who does the heavy lifting. We can open ourselves up to being God's instruments by prayer. Remember, prayer is effective and changes hearts. So, if we are not praying for our coworkers, we are not evangelizing them.

Once others know we are disciples of Jesus and we have earned the right to have conversations about faith, we can ask them what they would like us to pray for. Let them know that we will pray for them. If we feel called to go even further, we can ask them if they would be open to saying a prayer right then. Of course, it may not be prudent to do this in a staff meeting at an engineering firm, but if we have the opportunity to do so, take advantage of it.

THE WORKPLACE IS A MISSION FIELD

The office where I once worked was one of the most godless places I have ever experienced. There were hundreds of employees, but I was the only practicing Christian in the building that I knew of. This meant that if I did not evangelize, nobody would. My perspective changed when I started to consider my workplace as my mission field.

If you are a stay-at-home mother, you have a mission field in the world, too. You are bound to have interactions with non-Christians everywhere you go—on the playground, in the grocery store, at school functions or sporting events. No matter what your vocation, God has called you to a particular mission, in a particular location, in a particular time. The question is not if you ought to evangelize, but whom you ought to evangelize and how.

USE PRUDENCE

We have to make sure that evangelization, discussions about faith, and other personal matters never take away from our time fulfilling the duties we owe our employers. Lastly, if others tell us they do not want to talk about faith, we ought to respect their decisions and drop the subject, unless they bring it up later.

FEARS

Ultimately, going deeper into a relationship means we have to take some risks. There is a point where we have to risk talking about our faith. At this point, there is a choice. Do I risk rejection, hostility, and anger? I might keep a friend, but at what cost? If I talk about my faith, I risk a negative reaction and loss, but I also may gain salvation. We have to risk sacrificing the relationship.

Still, there are ways we can make the chance of rejection smaller, and that happens by being honest. Why not tell someone, "I really care about our friendship and am happy that we have become closer. As friends, can I be completely honest with you? I want to tell you about my relationship with Christ and how much it means to me." Then be quiet and see what the other person says. This kind of statement helps others know we care about them as friends, not just as check marks on our agenda.

John the Baptist was attempting to evangelize Herod, and Herod decided to have him killed. That is having trouble in evangelization. Paul was beaten, jailed, scoffed at, run out of towns, rejected, and ultimately killed for his evangelization. Why do we complain when others decide they don't like us? Evangelization costs us something. In fact, Jesus promised it.

Success is when we offer others Jesus, not just doctrines, programs, classes, retreats, or community. Now these things can be used as avenues to offer Jesus, but they can also become replacements for Jesus when we do not explicitly offer salvation through him.

Success in evangelization is being faithful to doing what Jesus asks of us. That means doing our best in evangelization and not being results-oriented. While this moderation of our understanding of success will help, we also need to expect that many will not be converted to Jesus just because we try to evangelize them. In other words, we will sometimes fail to help others come into a life-giving relationship with Jesus. Expecting failure can aid us as evangelists because it helps us understand we are not in charge and our failure can still be used by God for his glory.

Do we love others enough to evangelize explicitly? If not, then we do not love them enough.

PAUL WAS NOT ONLY

a bishop; he was a tentmaker. His vocation was to be part of the priesthood and leadership of the Church, but his trade was making tents. Even while traveling to different cities, Paul repeatedly tells us, he kept up his trade. In 1 Thessalonians 2, he says that he did not want to be a burden to others while sharing his life and the message of the gospel with others. He also speaks of toiling day and night in labor.

In his hard work he witnessed to something that his words could not. His work showed that he lived out what he professed. Paul

was a man of integrity, hard work, devotion, friendship, and zeal. He was not always the gentlest or nicest man, but his witness was effective enough to make him the great evangelist of the new Church. He did all of this in the midst of working hard in order to earn a living and show that work is valuable. We, too, can learn from Paul that our work has value and meaning. We, too, can bear witness to the love of God in and through our work. And we cannot fail to verbally witness to the Good News that we hold so dear when the opportunities arise at work.

QUESTIONS FOR CONSIDERATION

✳ *Name some coworkers whom you believe you may be called to evangelize.*

✳ *What are some of the ways you might share your faith with them?*

✳ *What is your internal reaction when you think about evangelizing these people?*

✳ *What barriers may block your ability to evangelize them?*

CHAPTER 11

SPIRITUAL MENTORS AND APPRENTICES

I thought I would retire from working in campus ministry. I already had fifteen years of full-time work with college students, and I loved it. But then I did something dangerous. I asked Jesus if he wanted something different from me. I asked him to show me his path. He did, and it eventually led me to start Catholic Missionary Disciples. For the last few years, I have been working with diocesan and parish teams to help them learn what I am sharing with you in this book as well as how to start the process of parish renewal. But that was not the only major change God had in store for me.

Because I was already beyond forty and more of a father figure than a peer to the young men I was mentoring, I prayed that God might show me if I was meant to sow seeds in another mission field. He did, and I started to do so. I felt called to start working with laymen who were similar to me in vocation. Thus, I started to invest more and more in husbands and fathers close to my age. I started by initiating more in friendships. Some men I knew well and others I didn't. Regardless, I stopped waiting for them to ask me to lunch and regularly reached out to them to get together. Then I started to really push beyond the normal conversations.

I started asking them big questions, including many of the ones you can find in this book. I asked questions such as "What do you want out of life?" and "How is your walk with God going?" It started to spur deeper conversations. I then asked them how their relationships with other men were. Most confided in me that they had few close friends and even their best friendships were not intentional enough when it came to discipleship. I asked them if they wanted more, and several responded that they did indeed want more.

I then offered a big vision. I asked them to pray about a two-year investment of time and effort. We would meet at least once a week to pray together, talk about things that really mattered, and then challenge one another. At the end of the first year, they would start to discern the men whom they could intentionally invest in themselves. Men who also needed the kind of community we would form.

Three other men eventually agreed to this process, and we started walking together with the goal of being better disciples. I had led such groups with many college-aged men through the years. Those college students are now doctors, teachers, engineers, husbands, fathers, and priests. Mentoring and "discipling" them taught me how to accompany others. I am now applying those principles to men closer to my age. I expect nothing less than for Jesus to make missionary disciples who make other missionary disciples, because we are meant to do discipleship alongside others, not by ourselves.

MENTORSHIP

Disciples make other disciples.

Mentors who apprentice others can then guide their apprentices to be mentors later on. Think of it this way. If you want to be a great artist, the best way to learn is to apprentice under a great artist. Want to be a great plumber? Apprentice under a great plumber. Want to be a great mom? Apprentice under a great mom.

Want to be a great Catholic? Our current methodology is through books, videos, classes, programs, and events. While these things are helpful, they cannot replace being an apprentice.

If we are good disciples, we help other disciples become mature. All the other methodologies can be avenues for good things to happen, but they cannot do what a mentor–apprentice relationship can. Jesus had no program. He had his mission, his vision, and his strategy. Programs can work if we adopt Jesus' mission, vision, and strategy. To quote the book of Hebrews, "And let us consider how to stir up one another to love and good works, not neglecting to meet together, as is the habit of some, but encouraging one another, and all the more as you see the Day drawing near" (Hebrews 10:24-25).

We need to activate the gifts, knowledge, and experiences of the older generations in order to reach the next generation. This is one of the strategies of God that is plain to see in the Scriptures. So many passed on their authority, wisdom, calling, and in some cases their vocation to those who could take their place. Moses and Joshua. Eli and

Samuel. Samuel and David. Elijah and Elisha. Jesus and the Twelve. Paul and Timothy. Paul and Titus.

MODERN SMALL GROUPS

With nearly two decades of full-time experience in Catholic ministry, I have seen thousands of small groups. Of these groups, I can tell you that only a few dozen have ever had a significant impact on the larger parish where I was working. If we look at average small groups in average Catholic parishes, we see they are pretty similar from place to place. They last for a time (some for many years), but they are not leading to substantial transformation of the lives of nonbelievers, and rarely do they help form Catholics into disciples who evangelize others.

This is because too many small groups are holy huddles. People might individually grow, but they do not share what they have received with people outside of their small group. Yet small groups are not meant to be holy huddles.

Now, to model our small groups on a modern method that leads to lasting transformation, we ought to look at twelve-step groups. The record of transformation has been proven by the success stories of organizations such as Alcoholics Anonymous. They work because there is clarity in the process, transformed lives are their purpose, they guide all participants through a way to achieve transformation, they have built-in accountability, they teach humility, they demand honesty, and they have built-in replicability.

I made the biggest jump in learning how to help others grow closer to Jesus while working with sex addicts in groups based on the twelve steps. Within a month of starting my work with college students, I had the first man struggling with sex addiction walk into my office. He told me he was looking at pornography, masturbating, and could not stop. He wanted my help. I honestly did not know what to do. I sought help with Catholic resources, but there weren't any at the time. I finally called the addiction studies department at the local university. They connected me with two professors who were studying sex addiction.

We met, and they recommended some strategies I could use. They also said that there was a doctoral student who needed some counseling hours with whom I might partner. We started a group based on the twelve steps of recovery. I also implemented a Catholic understanding of sexuality into the group, especially through St. John Paul II's Theology of the Body. I learned a lot by messing up. And yet God changed lives, and I grew as a disciple maker and mentor of others.

Twelve-step groups can be rather blunt and impolite places. There is a kind of desperation that infects the groups, rather than the comfort of what happens in most Catholic small groups. It is actually refreshing because you skip all the fluff and talk about things that matter. I fit right in since I am a blunt communicator myself. Being anonymous really helps, too, because people have an opportunity to truly let down their guard. In contrast, in most Catholic small groups, we feel we still have to put on a show in order to hide our true struggles, wounds, sin, and problems. We want to appear to be the person who has it all together when we see each other during Mass. But that person is not real, in many ways. We are sinners. We have problems. We need others.

We compartmentalize our lives too much. Too often we put on the mask of being a "good Catholic." Twelve-step groups break this down. They go right to the problem and face it head-on. We Catholics rarely do this in small groups; instead, a typical Catholic group is more like a polite dinner party among acquaintances than a place for Christian accountability with friends where we lay out our raw souls.

We need groups that lead to transformed lives and mission. Change is not merely about *knowing* the right doctrine (though this is important). It is about *living* a life that is pleasing to God. Certainly, we need to learn and think rightly. But growing as a disciple of Jesus primarily is done by reorienting our actions and habits toward God. Instead of "what do you think about _____" questions, we ought to ask questions about prayer, sabbath rest, fasting, sinful desires, temptations, relationships, growth in virtue, and how we are going to grow in our discipleship.

The success of a twelve-step group lies in going through each step with the help of a small group and a sponsor. Imagine a Catholic small group where we had tangible markers for a disciple (pray every day, go to confession every four weeks, begin to evangelize, etc.) and each marker or step was nonnegotiable. Knowing the steps and doing them are two very different things. The doing is awfully difficult, and we need to acknowledge that.

Some other insights from twelve-step groups may help us understand how to run our own small groups. First of all, we cannot build intimacy unless we spend time together. If a recovering drug addict has one priority, it is being sober. Our one priority should be to become saints who get ourselves and others to heaven. If this is the case, then we will make the time to meet with others. The significance of it all can be summed up this way: an addict cares more about sobriety than most Catholics do about Jesus' mission to save the world.

Furthermore, the meetings are simple and repeatable. No one needs to have expertise to lead a discussion, read from a book, or say a simple prayer. Anybody who has participated in a twelve-step group will tell you that it is a simple affair, but that transformation is found in the relationships and the support of having one another invested in the group. Participants want to change.

FIVE ESSENTIAL ELEMENTS FOR SMALL GROUPS

With all of this in mind, we can see that many of our small groups need radical renewal. Here are five elements that can start the change.

1. Having vision. Small-group leaders must know the purpose of the small group. They also must be able to tell group member what is going to take place in the next "generation" of small groups. In short, no group is an end unto itself. They need to be able to prepare the members to build more small groups.

Some groups have been in existence for a long time. The members gain more and more knowledge of Church teachings and the Bible, but often their personal prayer, actions, and mission stay the same during that time. Mostly that is because the group is fulfilling its purpose: education on specific subjects. That's fine, but the groups have not become change agents in the lives of group members so they can help improve the lives of those outside the current groups. In order to change others' lives, we must first experience change in our own lives.

2. Intentionally aiming at making disciples. Can we name the disciples we have made? Do we know how to make a disciple? Most Christians do not know how to make a disciple and cannot name one they have made. That is a trumpet call to change! It means we can do better. Remember, our mission is to fulfill Jesus' call to "make disciples." God wants to reach others through us. There is no doubt about that. The process starts with being intentional about what we do to make disciples. Get better at the practical skills described in this book. Ask someone to hold us accountable to acting with intention. Such spadework can have a great effect on the results of what we do. Leadership is the main ingredient. Without it, most groups cannot achieve their goal.

3. Aiming for conversion. Too much of discipleship and ministry is about receiving information passively. Our aim must be transformation that stems from the conversion of heart and action. Information remains important because we cannot love what we do not know. Think of knowledge as a tool to help us love more. We must continually strive to be converted more fully into the people God calls us to be. This will only happen when we open our own hearts in prayer and let the Holy Spirit work through us.

4. Being honest and vulnerable. Few people are comfortable sharing their deepest secrets, especially with a stranger. That's natural. It takes time, energy, and trust to build relationships that are intimate enough that we are comfortable sharing. But that is important because surface-level chats won't get us far. The keys to building vulnerability are praying together, asking tough questions, holding one another accountable, and being patient with the group.

Humility also is vital. Many will not be open with others because of pride. They think others will think less of them for being imperfect. Not so. When a friend confides in you about an area he or she is struggling with and asks for assistance, do you think less of that person? Of course not. It's likely you think more highly of the person for humbly trying to grow. The same goes for each of us. Vulnerability can be positive.

5. Following a process that can be replicated. In today's Catholic Church in America, we have failed to remember a lot of what made us missionaries. Few of us had another person come with us on the journey to Christian maturity, so we need help. A curriculum or a process that can teach ways of evangelization and discipleship can help. Some mature disciples may not need such help, but Christians with less experience assuredly will. To reproduce the evangelization and discipleship process in others so it does not need expert Christian leaders means we need a simple process that can be replicated so we can teach it to others.

PAUL LEARNED

how to be a disciple from the Jewish rabbi Gamaliel. Rabbis of his time would invite potential disciples to follow them. This meant both rabbis and their disciples spent part of the time working in order to support themselves and spent the rest of their time together. Disciples would learn how to teach the Scriptures, travel with their rabbi, eat with him, and even mimic his habits. To follow meant to imitate.

Paul started to take on disciples as well. He traveled with Barnabas, Timothy, Luke, and Titus. He taught them how to lead. He showed them how to evangelize and teach. He shared his life with them and told them to imitate him in how he lived his life. This is the biblical model of discipleship. We may not be able to work part-time and mentor part-time, but we can still imitate the model of Jesus, Paul, and the other apostles. We can learn how to be a disciple by being disciples of more mature Catholics and then having disciples of our own once we are ready to lead others.

QUESTIONS FOR CONSIDERATION

✳ *Do you know more mature Catholics whom you are following?*

✳ *If not, how might you seek out such a relationship?*

✳ *If you do know more mature Catholics, how is the relationship leading you to be a better disciple of Jesus?*

✳ *Are you ready to invite others to be your disciples?*

✳ *If you do not feel ready, in what area do you need to grow?*

CHAPTER 12

TRUST, VULNERABILITY, INTIMACY, ACCOUNTABILITY

I recall the first time I told my wife I loved her. I was terrified. We had dated for a while, and I was totally in love with her. She had won my heart, but I was fighting with myself over whether I should tell her how I felt. *I have everything to lose*, I thought. If I told her of my love for her and she rejected me, I would be hurt. I had been hurt in previous relationships and had some pretty low self-esteem at the time.

But I also thought, *The risk is worth the reward. And she may be waiting for me to take the first step. If so, then our relationship will take the next step.* I gathered up the courage to tell her I loved her. She responded, and the rest is family history.

To be vulnerable opens us to possible harm or risk. It arises from our limitations and weaknesses. Every time we admit that we are weak, we take a risk. But we all are imperfect. All of us sin. We fail. We do some things wrong. Mistakes abound. We hurt God, others, and ourselves. We are flawed. Our wounds show. Admitting such things takes courage. Being vulnerable takes courage. When we fear admitting our weakness, we often cannot grow. That is why we must be vulnerable to God and a few others.

But before we can be vulnerable with God and people, we must have a basic form of trust. That is usually easier said than done. In the minds of some Christians, becoming vulnerable with God should be easy for all people because God is the only really trustworthy one in our lives. That is true objectively, but the personal, subjective side may be harder to see. Some have false images of God. Some don't trust anyone. Some don't believe God is real. There are many barriers to trusting God and many barriers to trusting other people. But we still need to try to do it. Remember, the real birthplace of intimacy is vulnerability. Without intimacy, building relationships with others is impossible. Here is the pattern:

Trust → Vulnerability → Intimacy → Accountability

The result of such a way of operating is that we can form deep relationships and grow in love. Thus, if we want a life of loving relationships, we have to start with trust that builds vulnerability.

I ought to note that the vulnerability I am referring to is not counseling or therapy. Vulnerability is not just sharing emotions, nor is it dumping our baggage. It is not telling our darkest secrets. It is not confessing all our sins to a friend. It is not letting each other become victims. Instead, vulnerability comes from love and is expressed in the safety of real, trusting relationships. Vulnerability is allowing others to know our real selves and pulling off the masks that we hide behind. We allow others to see our gifts, weaknesses, wounds, virtues, and struggles. It is allowing ourselves to be seen and loved for who we truly are, not putting up masks.

When we are able to be vulnerable, we can start being accountable to each other. Accountability does not mean another person tells us all our faults and how to fix them and then makes us do it. Rather, accountability starts with humility, recognizing areas of our lives where we need to grow. Then we share these areas with others, along with achievable goals that we want to set for ourselves, in order to try to grow. After this, the other person will help remind us of our goals, check in on how we are doing, support us, and gently challenge us if necessary. That is accountability born out of love for one another with the goal of helping each other become saints.

FRIENDSHIP AND LOVE

From that point, we build trust and friendship that is deep. This can lead into *agape*, the highest type of love. That is the kind of love that is intentional and strives for the things that are best for the other, despite any cost to self. Vulnerability enables us to admit we are imperfect and that others are, as well, while accepting that others and we remain worthy of love.

When we are vulnerable, a relationship has space for these features:

- Confession to each other of sins so we can work on virtue together.

- A life with more virtue, born out of shared accountability.

- Humility.

- Perseverance when suffering.

- Empathy with others who suffer.

- Greater kindness.

- Courageously acknowledging our weakness and growing from it.

- Allowing others to relate better to us and vice versa.

This is why discipleship requires vulnerability. Vulnerability is the shortcut to loving God more and helping others do likewise. To take that shortcut, we have to risk letting others see our weaknesses. We have to have courage and be humble enough to let others see our real selves, even if it might mean we get hurt emotionally. True discipleship can never reach full flower until we have the types of deep relationships that seek the good of others.

See what St. Paul says about this in 2 Corinthians 12:7-10. In this passage he speaks of his suffering, which he wants God to take away, yet which remains. This has led Paul to see that it is through his weakness that God can be strong. Therefore Paul does not rely on his own strength but the strength of God to get him through. This must have been humbling for Paul to admit.

Notice the apostle's vulnerability here. He admits his struggles. This imitates Jesus, who showed one hundred percent vulnerability on the Cross. Jesus was tempted, felt sad, and got angry. He felt pain emotionally. He did not want to suffer, but he did so anyway. Why? He loved us more than he feared pain and death. Jesus' whole life models vulnerability for us. He spent time with outcasts. He washed feet, a very humble act. He interacted with and touched lepers. He opposed injustices. He took social norms and turned them upside down.

Being vulnerable with God and others is risky, but the reward is worth it. When a leader shows he or she is vulnerable, it permits others to do the same. It fosters connection and growth. Jesus was the perfect model for this. Now we have to do it for other people.

To quote C. S. Lewis,

> To love at all is to be vulnerable. Love anything, and your heart will certainly be wrung and possibly be broken. If you want to make sure of keeping it intact, you must give your heart to no one, not even to an animal. Wrap it carefully round with hobbies and little luxuries; avoid all entanglements; lock it up safe in the casket or coffin of your selfishness. But in that casket—safe, dark, motionless, airless—it will change. It will not be broken; it will become unbreakable, impenetrable, irredeemable. The alternative to tragedy, or at least to the risk of tragedy, is damnation. The only place outside Heaven where you can be perfectly safe from all the dangers and perturbations of love is Hell.[26]

FRIENDS AND DISCIPLES TOGETHER

This may have been the best compliment I ever got. I had been mentoring a young man. One day he told me, "Until I met you, I never knew what it meant to have a father love a son. Now I see, through you, how much God loves me." I was floored, humbled, and overjoyed at God's work in this discipleship relationship.

Of course, we didn't get there right away. We invested time with each other. We had coffee together. We shared drinks and meals. We texted all the time. We prayed together and challenged each other to grow spiritually. We laughed and had fun. Working side by side, he became my spiritual son.

Those are some of the marks of a good discipleship relationship. Think of it as an apprenticeship in the life of following Jesus. To quote the United States Conference of Catholic Bishops (USCCB):

> To create a culture of witness, we must live explicit lives of discipleship. Being a disciple is a challenge. Fortunately, one does not become a disciple of Christ on his or her own initiative. The work of the Holy Spirit within the Christian community forms the person as a disciple of Christ. One seeking to learn how to be a disciple of Christ does so through apprenticeship. ... Apprenticeship "links an experienced Christian believer, or mentor, with one who seeks a deeper relationship with Christ and the Church." Furthermore, this relationship is a "guided encounter with the entire Christian life, a journey toward conversion to Christ. It is a school for discipleship that promotes an authentic following of Christ based on the acceptance of one's baptismal responsibilities, the internalization of the word of God, and the transformation of the whole person to 'life in Christ.'" Apprenticeship is an essential element in witnessing to the Gospel message.[27]

That is a great vision for discipleship and accompaniment. The process is inefficient and could be long—it might take years. That's fine. Jesus spent three years with his disciples.

It is sad we don't have many such relationships in the Church these days. I took an unscientific poll of leaders in Catholic evangelization, and only a handful have ever had discipleship relationships. And these are the best-of-the-best leaders in evangelization. This is why not many Catholics have experienced a discipleship relationship. Few were mentored, so we can't blame them for never mentoring.

When we do not have disciple makers who know how to equip others to evangelize, it is no wonder that so few Catholics are sharing their faith. Herein lies the crux of our problems: a lack of discipleship relationships that lead to missionary disciples making other missionary disciples.

How did Jesus express his love for his disciples? He lived with them for three years, getting to know them deeply, teaching them, and being an example to them of how to live as disciples. He was vulnerable with them. He held them accountable. He challenged them. He trained them. He forgave them. He apprenticed them. He modeled appropriate intimacy. He was their leader. And then, he commissioned them to do the same thing with others.

To grow most naturally as disciples, we can sit at the feet of a mature disciple and let that mentor lead and be our role model. The *Catechism* speaks of this in strong terms: "The disciple of Christ must not only keep the faith and live on it, but also profess it, confidently bear witness to it, and spread it. ... Service of and witness to the faith are necessary for salvation" (CCC 1816).

We must have help to put such a vision in practice in our lives. To be successful disciples and teach others, we need someone to help us learn what Jesus and the Catholic Church call us to do. To "disciple" others, we need to be "discipled" too.

There are no quick fixes in discipleship, and it is hard work. But God created us to do it. We are not meant to be disciples of Jesus by ourselves.

JESUS WEPT

at the tomb of Lazarus. This show of emotion and mourning is a great example of Jesus being vulnerable to those around him, because the Bible tells us that Jesus loved Lazarus greatly. The disciples of Jesus did not know Lazarus as Jesus did, so while they were probably sad that he had died, they would not have felt such a rush of grief. Jesus shows that it is not only normal but good to miss those whom you love.

Jesus' relationship with these three siblings was very deep. We can see that Jesus felt secure enough in the relationship to challenge Martha after she complained that Mary was not helping her with the household chores. They must have had great intimacy, built up over years of being friends. Friends who trusted each other. Friends who were vulnerable. Friends who held each other accountable. Friends who loved one another.

QUESTIONS FOR CONSIDERATION

✳ *What holds you back from trusting others?*
Have you been hurt by others in the past?

✳ *Are you free to be vulnerable with your friends*
and family? Why or why not?

✳ *Do you have opportunities to be intimate and accountable to others who are trying to be good disciples of Jesus?*

✳ *If not, how could you start to work on these kinds of relationships?*

CHAPTER 13

WORLDVIEW AND CATHOLIC IDENTITY

Have you ever heard someone say, "Well, that might be true for you but not for me." I certainly have, and it drives me bananas. This is because I believe relativism (the belief that truth is relative to culture, people, or situations) is false, and sometimes I struggle to connect with people who are moral relativists. As a result, I had to change my approach to be a more effective evangelizer.

After realizing I was having a tough time understanding today's logic of relativism (or its lack of logic), I decided to simply listen and learn. I decided that to reach the heart of the one I was talking with, I had to know how the individual worked out this way of thinking. You cannot love what you don't know, so learning what made a person tick was important. I also remembered that understanding someone does not mean accepting his or her beliefs. Lastly, I learned much more with my mouth shut and my ears open, though that is still a work in progress.

Perhaps you have run across similar conversation roadblocks with those who do not think as you do. Perhaps you are getting nowhere as an evangelist. Here are a few thoughts on why Catholics talk past people they are trying to evangelize in today's world.

1. We use the same words but speak different languages. When we use Catholic terms or any faith-based words, the meaning may be totally different in the mind of the other person. For instance, *Church, love, peace, faith,* and *God* can have different definitions. What do we mean when we use them? What do others mean? Clarity is crucial, so we must define our words. But to get to know how another thinks, we have to listen and ask good questions, as we outlined earlier in the book.

2. We fail to listen for what is blocking a person's path to faith and think we already know. Many Catholics who are asked why a person left the Church will typically say the individual "wasn't catechized well" or "didn't understand the Faith." Maybe yes, maybe no. If no one talked with the person leaving the Church, how do we know? Ask, listen, and understand. I know many people who left the Church who knew the Faith well, so no one could say they weren't properly catechized or taught correctly. Why did they stop attending Mass? They were burned out. They were lonely. Every one of the people I talked with over the last year left for reasons that had nothing to do with theology or the sacraments. Of course, many do leave for theological reasons or are not catechized well. But do not fill in the blanks for others in the search for reasons.

When we supply the answers without asking enough questions, we tend to drive people away. We might tell them what they should value, want, and do, and that ministry model is broken. Instead, we must seek to understand, serve, and love the people we are talking with before we offer solutions. Build a relationship first, and then invoke sound preaching and correction.

3. Many active Catholics and other Christians have no non-Christian friends. No matter how motivated we are to evangelize, we will be unable to evangelize non-Christians well if we don't have meaningful relationships with them. Who are we evangelizing with intention right now? If we cannot answer that, our first step may well be to ask a coworker or a neighbor to go out for coffee.

4. The lens we see the world through is political, not Catholic. It is important to remember that no politician or political party reflects a Catholic view of the world perfectly. When we conflate Christianity with politics, we can pervert the gospel. Gospel values sometimes intersect with politics, but don't confuse the two. If our world were to follow all of Jesus' teachings, what would that look like? Politics does not give us the answer. While it is fine to be involved politically or work for political answers to cultural and moral problems, we should avoid the temptation to substitute political views for faith or faith for politics. Seeing the world through a political lens damages our witness to others, too. It's likely that we will disagree at some point with another's political point of view on any number of issues, even if we agree with the values behind the issues. Such disagreements, if we confuse the religious principle with the political method, keep us from witnessing to the gospel and delivering truth to others.

A CATHOLIC WORLDVIEW

Understanding a worldview helps us understand where someone else is coming from. Knowing the lens through which someone else sees the world will help us to help that person. The trick is that there is just one way to know a person's view of the world, and that is to listen. Be an interested friend who asks lots of questions, and you will gain understanding of that person. That means investing yourself and taking the time, placing your own wants and needs in the background.

Some equate evangelization with having the right answer every time. I used to be like that. (My kids might say I still am.) I tried to evangelize by winning arguments or proving another person wrong. I wasted time repelling others with my pride and lack of love before I woke up and saw the error of my ways. Apologetics or a solid argument for your point of view can be used to help someone overcome an objection and become closer to Jesus, but it rarely brings anyone closer to him on its own.

Some think our faith is private and should be kept to ourselves so we aren't perceived as offensive. That's the Catholic "don't ask, don't tell." Such a philosophy is born in an environment that sees faith as a part-time hobby or something we compartmentalize. This fosters a culture of silence where faith is not discussed. Others have said, and I will repeat, that our faith is personal but never private.

What if the apostles had kept quiet about their faith? Christianity would not exist today.

I have found that the best way to evangelize is first to listen well to where others are spiritually. Listen to accept the person in front of you as God does, not to prove him or her wrong. Recognize that God made that unique person in his image, for his glory. When we listen and accept another like this, we can love that person as God does and establish a foundation to help that person grow. True love for others means seeking their good. Ask probing questions to learn how to help spark that growth.

All of the strategies mentioned in this book build on a Catholic worldview, which is always based on the gospel. Our view of the world is revealed in Christ. Seeing the world through the eyes of Jesus clears everything up: our purpose, our mission to make disciples, our identity and the identity of others as children of God. Ultimately, the goal of our evangelizing is to help people see the world through the eyes of our Lord. To do that, we have to see the world that way, too.

SOFT-SELLING CATHOLICISM

Being a faithful Catholic in the United States in the twenty-first century is not easy. Scandals coupled with declining and vanishing parishes afflict us. While we have a legion of problems, they are just symptoms of a deep issue. Too many Catholics are pursuing false gods instead of Jesus. These gods have many appearances: wealth, pleasure, comfort, and worldly success.

This is our own fault, in large part. Our Catholic culture soft-sells Catholicism, holiness, evangelization, and discipleship.

Our radical view of the world and our doctrines, practices, and disciplines have been given an easier aspect that the world is more ready to approve. Since Catholicism is so radical, some Catholics have desired to make it easier to accept by undercutting the more challenging parts of our Faith. That means only allowing Jesus to be Lord of the portions of our lives we are comfortable letting him lead.

That does not work. Christianity is supposed to be radical, and Jesus wants to be Lord of one hundred percent of our lives. Plainly stated, Jesus came here as a human, suffered, died, and rose again to be Lord of all of our lives, not so we could be comfortable, have a lot of worldly goods, or be self-satisfied.

Jesus entered this world with a higher purpose, and that was to reconcile us to the Father, forgive us, heal our wounds, and give us life everlasting. Let someone else be a life coach, a mere miracle worker, a pal. We can find our own social workers, counselors, and doctors. We need Jesus to be exactly what he is: God, Lord, Savior, Messiah, Light of the World, and the only path to salvation.

We Catholics should cease remaking Jesus into what we want him to be and let him be who he is. That is one important way to help the Church recover her ability to bring salvation to this world. In short, we must stop soft-selling Christianity to ourselves first and then others. God is God. Jesus is Lord. And we are his disciples. Let's be true disciples and servants following the Master.

THE LOOK OF TRUE DISCIPLESHIP

As true disciples of Jesus, we are called now to focus on the challenging subjects, not avoid them. Christianity done right is never easy. We have tried the easy path, and it leads nowhere. It has failed the world. It has failed us.

Jesus called us Catholics—you and me—to be the world's light and salt. If we fail, our world has no chance of salvation. Jesus has no plan B to make up for the failures of his Church—you and me. We are supposed to be instruments of salvation. If we don't act as those instruments, the world will go to hell. Literally.

We need no more somber saints, hesitant disciples, cultural Catholics, or comfy Christians. No more Catholic buzzwords or gadgets or meetings or unreadable documents.

Instead, we need witnesses who are radical, who have died to themselves so Christ can reign in them. We need people to evangelize and make disciples. We must have prayer warriors and real saints. We need people willing to die—figuratively or literally—so others have a chance to live forever.

DYING TO OURSELVES

We might think we know the issues of the world, but they are not drugs, sex, pop culture, or politics. The world's problems are in the sinful hearts of people who have not turned over their lives to God. Thus, the answer is located in the polar opposite of a sinful heart—one filled with the grace, peace, and mercy of God. A heart sold on Jesus. This is the heart of a missionary disciple. God wants us to die and then be reborn to a new life in him.

To truly die to ourselves, we must become uncomfortable. We must reach society's fringes with the gospel. That will change the world. It's not a class, a program, or an event.

It is the gospel of Jesus Christ. Jesus risked his life for the gospel's sake. He was hated and killed for it.

At the same time, Jesus respected the free will of others. He let folks walk off if they would not accept his message. He let them walk away when they found it too challenging or difficult. What about us? Do we accept Jesus' words? Do we have enough courage to say tough things to others like Jesus did?

We may say, "Sure!" After all, we're pro-life, pro-marriage, pro-family. But hold on. Is that enough? Listen to the Master:

> Now great multitudes accompanied him; and he turned and said to them, "If any one comes to me and does not hate his own father and mother and wife and children and brothers and sisters, yes, and even his own life, he cannot be my disciple. Whoever does not bear his own cross and come after me, cannot be my disciple. For which of you, desiring to build a tower, does not first sit down and count the cost, whether he has enough to complete it? Otherwise, when he has laid a foundation, and is not able to finish, all who see it begin to mock him, saying, 'This man began to build, and was not able to finish.' Or what king, going to encounter another king in war, will not sit down first and take counsel whether he is able with ten thousand to meet him who comes against him with twenty thousand? And if not, while the other is yet a great way off, he sends an embassy and asks terms of peace. So therefore, whoever of you does not renounce all that he has cannot be my disciple." (Luke 14:25-33)

See the large crowds? Perhaps these are like the masses that come to church on Sunday. I have a hunch the disciples were thinking, "We have something going! A movement! Real numbers are coming to our events." Imagine those words being preached in your parish. Would they be received with enthusiasm or hostility? Remember, some wanted Jesus dead because of his message, yet we worry what others might think of us if we simply mention the name of Jesus to them.

Think about why the Catholic Church in the West is declining rapidly. Why is it so hard for us to reach many people? Well, do we resemble Jesus and his disciples in our words and lives? Do we look like the great saints who helped renew the Church during their years?

Jesus' message is tough and not supposed to be diluted. His message must transform us and then be lived in a radical way by those who call themselves Catholic. We need to act like Jesus and sound more like him. We need more courage to be Catholic. The world has turned its back on the soft-sell of following Jesus. Let us give others something completely different: Jesus' Cross—where bad news loses and Good News wins in the end.

Jesus' message was true two thousand years ago when he preached it, and it is true and fresh today. Therefore, his followers must live according to these truths. If we are supposed to live by the words of our Lord, why does his Church act so differently today?

Let us return to Jesus' gospel message, the heart of our Faith, and use the word of God to change our own hearts and then the hearts of others.

PAUL HAD TO BE

taken to Athens because his life was in danger due to his efforts to evangelize. Paul stayed in Athens while awaiting the arrival of Silas and Timothy, who had remained in Berea to minister to the community. While traveling in Athens, Paul became distressed because there were so many idols in the city. One day, some Stoic philosophers heard Paul preaching and brought him to the Areopagus, where various philosophers would debate the merits of their ideas. Paul used it as an opportunity to preach the gospel. Knowing his audience, he understood that quoting Jewish scripture to them would not help. They did not believe in it. Furthermore, they were highly educated, so he would have to use an argument that was persuasive.

Paul decided to use their local idol worship as part of his argument. He said that he noticed one idol to an unknown god. He used this as a segue to teach them about who Jesus is and how he rose from the dead to save us. Due to his preaching, some Greeks became Christians, though we do not know if any of the philosophers converted. Paul tailored his message to the worldview he encountered in Athens. We should do the same while bringing the gospel to our own time and setting.

QUESTIONS FOR CONSIDERATION

✳ *Do you have non-Catholic friends? If so, what are some ways you can start to pop the Catholic bubble?*

✳ *In what ways have you settled in your faith life? Humbly examine your conscience for areas where you have not grown. Write them down.*

✳ *What parts of your worldview fail to match the worldview of Jesus and his Church?*

✳ *How can you start to develop a more Catholic worldview?*

CHAPTER 14

BARRIERS TO SUCCESS AND NEXT STEPS

My toe hurt so badly, I could hardly walk. Continuing to train for a marathon was out of the question. The toe swelled up to about two times its normal size. I saw a podiatrist, who said the issue was overtraining. He gave me shots and prescribed medicine that helped in the short run, but he misdiagnosed the illness. Much later, a rheumatologist correctly diagnosed me with psoriatic arthritis. He found a treatment plan that worked.

A misdiagnosis can mean that an illness gets treated incorrectly. That can make the illness worse. In several ways, that is what is happening in our Church's parishes and dioceses. The symptoms of what's wrong are clear—declining memberships, a loss of influence, fewer men and women choosing a religious vocation. But many have misdiagnosed the illness. We blame the symptoms on issues like bad catechizing, clericalism, loss of reverence, immoral behavior, or the sexual revolution. Those issues are important, but they are not the underlying illness.

One way we diagnose our illness incorrectly is blaming Catholic institutions such as diocesan offices, parishes, schools, and hospitals. Those structures are not the place to look. The problems stem from failing to understand our mission or implement a proper strategy. Most of the diocesan and parish leaders I work with want to be more fruitful. They desire to evangelize, lead, and form missionary disciples, but they face huge obstacles. In some cases, institutional thinking is part of the problem, but that often is a symptom of a deeper illness.

Some illnesses the Church is currently suffering from include:

1. Catholic Identity Sickness – Many think the Church's reason for being is to maintain the structures it has created. Others think the Church exists for other purposes, such as giving us the sacraments, feeding the poor, teaching correct doctrine, and so on. All are important, but the Catholic Church exists for one reason: to evangelize. Our job is to make disciples. When we fail to do this, we can lapse into a maintenance mode, losing our true identity. Our structures are intended to support our identity and mission, not replace them. Identity sickness is healed by returning to mission. To diagnose whether our parish or diocese suffers from this sickness, look at where the priorities are placed in budget, staffing, and scheduling.

2. The Wrong Strategy Disease – The Church does not exist to run programs. If we have the wrong strategy, we wind up replacing the strategy of Jesus with events, programs, and classes. Not enough Church leaders actually believe a big investment in a few people was Jesus' strategy. But the evidence says it is. Jesus knew what he was doing. Many Church leaders act like they know better than Jesus, and they have become managers of a parish organization, not fruitful evangelists who live lives as disciples. The "invest-in-the-crowds" strategy has failed. Jesus' strategy changed the culture. That can happen again.

3. This-Is-What-We-Know Disorder – This sickness results from a lack of faith and courage to operate outside our comfort zone. We don't want to be uncomfortable, so we avoid things outside our zone. We thwart our ability to grow and help others grow because we won't risk rejection in relationships or in our work. God wants his Church renewed more than we do. God wants us to go boldly and courageously. He waits for somebody to take a risk for him! Someone has to take the lead. Observe the saints. They did not become holy by being OK with the status quo. They ventured outside their comfort zone and were willing to operate differently. Renewal demands vision, courage, and leadership to move beyond what is comfortable and toward God's vision.

4. Wrong Understanding of Discipleship Sickness – The Church is using the correct words, including *discipleship, missionary disciples, evangelization, accompaniment,* and more. We talk well. But we need to understand that leading someone to convert, or merely making a disciple, is not the ultimate target. Our goal is to make disciples of people who then make disciples, who then make more disciples. It is spiritual multiplication. We never stop with converting one person to Jesus.

We work until we are all evangelists for Christ who then can make more disciples. Bare minimum doesn't work. Our leaders need to hear from us that evangelization and discipleship have to be big. Shoot for a big goal, the target Jesus set for us. Jesus did not stop with converting twelve men as disciples. He sent them to make more disciples and do as he did. They then deeply invested in other people and sent them out to make missionary disciples. What about us? How do we define success?

5. Creeping Universalism Disorder – If we fail to believe hell is an actual possibility for a person, or we fail to believe Jesus is the only path to salvation, we will not be evangelists. Many Catholics today believe and act as universalists or semi-universalists. They do not fully believe heaven, hell, and salvation are what the Church says they are. If we fully believe in salvation through Christ by faith, hope, and love and if we fully believe that heaven is real and that the grace of God through faith is the path to heaven, we should be spreading those truths to everyone. Hanging on to a form of universalism blocks our incentive to evangelize.

6. The Staff Does It All Sickness – This can also be called the Professionalism Infection. This is when Catholics allow the clergy, religious, and lay parish workers to do all the evangelization and discipleship work for them. Many times, the symptoms are found when we do not have an evangelization lifestyle but only try to evangelize when we are within the safety of the parish walls. The cure for this sickness is to help average Catholics become saints and evangelists who share the vision of Jesus.

7. Fearing Humans More Than God Infection – If there is one thing that holds many Catholics back from being bolder evangelists, it is fearing the reaction of others. The symptoms of this are biting our tongues when we feel called to speak up. It might mean we have good intentions that we rarely follow through on. It usually leads to shallow interactions with other Christians and few conversions of nonbelievers.

These underlying illnesses are not the only sources of our problems, but they are at the root of them. Start working on curing these illnesses. These countermeasures can lead us to become a body of Christ that is healthier than ever before.

THE PARISH

Few trends can solve problems by themselves. However, I am fully in favor of Catholic leaders who are trying to lead better. The current push to improve organizational practices is a superb idea. We do need better vision, planning, teamwork, meetings, and more. But there is a problem that gets a lot of private discussion, and we need to give it air publicly.

We will not solve the Church's problems by only developing better leadership skills and improving our organizational practices. We do need to get better at both because those improvements can help us give parishes and other Church structures a better chance to thrive. But to renew the Church, we must also renew the way we operate in evangelization and discipleship.

Better communications, meetings, vision, and so on are good, but without changing the way we evangelize and make disciples of others, all we will be doing is a more efficient job of managing decline. So, in addition to improving our organizational practices, we also have to improve our pastoral ways of operating.

Improving organizations with more effective teamwork and communication and better accountability is good. But it must be coupled with learning what is really needed to make everyday Catholics into disciples and to help those disciples make more disciples.

One without the other will not work. To get to real revival and growth, both must work hand in glove. To prove my opinion, read these examples (no names given). They are based on real cases in parishes I have seen that did one without the other.

Case #1 – Leadership Without Renewal of Pastoral Practices

In this parish, the leaders went to a great leadership conference. They returned with a renewed idea of what is needed to help a team grow in a healthy way, communicate better with each other, and collaborate. They built a team based on trust, an excellent thing for them to experience.

A year later, the internal health of the staff is better, but there is little fruitful change in their parish. Yes, they started a program that has led to some conversions, but some frustration is beginning to show. They see that the changes have made their work more efficient and stronger, but the parish has not moved forward. It has fallen back into conventional fixes: programs, classes, and events. They are frustrated because they have not sparked renewal as they hoped.

Case #2 – Renewal of Pastoral Practices Without Leadership

A similar problem is facing another parish: slow decline. The staff opted to work on changing how they operated pastorally. They made changes in which each staffer committed to prayer and then began to grow personally as an evangelist and maker of disciples. Each one began seeing more fruit in his or her personal apostolate. Yet, they did not achieve systematic change.

A few years later, the internal problems of money quarrels, staff compartmentalization, poor internal communication, meetings with no purpose, little visionary leadership, and other matters have kept the staff from working well together. Church politics can be ugly, and that is the case in this parish. In spite of a shared desire to change, this parish does not have the teamwork, honesty in communicating with each other, or leadership needed to work on matters together. Thus, they stay compartmentalized. They don't make sweeping changes, even if each person is a better individual evangelist.

Our conclusion is clear: Never try to do one without the other. We need both to successfully change cultures. Patience is required because this process is not easy or quick. Be humble. No individual has all the answers, but our wider universal Church does. Look for help when it's needed. Sometimes it's easier for an outsider like me to speak boldly about these matters. Do not settle for a quick fix, including this book.

Remember to pray. This is not a display of willpower and talent. It is about letting the Holy Spirit move in and through us.

Finally, now is the best time to start. The opportunity is presenting itself today. Grab it!

THE LAST WORD

During the time in which the Bible was written, one of the worst tragedies for a woman was to be unable to have children. A major scriptural theme is regaining fertility by God's gift. Infertility was a heavy trial. But God does not let anything go to waste, even our trials and suffering.

These principles apply now, too. God wants us to be fruitful spiritually. He wants us, whether individuals, families, or communities, to beget spiritual children. But many Catholics live spiritually barren lives, as do many parishes and dioceses. However, everything can be used as a tool for us to grow in holiness and in mission. The stories in the Bible show this truth.

Sarah and Abraham – Faith Overcomes Doubt

Sarah is the first person in the Bible with infertility. God does not let this be the end of the story. He promises early in the story that he will bless this couple—Abraham and Sarah—with offspring (see Genesis 12:7). God repeats this promise, but Sarah thinks God is acting too slowly, so she and Abraham come up with an idea to have Abraham get a servant pregnant. While Sarah fails to have faith in God, our Creator does not abandon her. Ultimately, he blesses Sarah and Abraham with a son, fulfilling his promise, albeit not in the time frame Sarah had in mind. A lesson here is that God's promises always lead to a better outcome than our own plans.

The Catholic Church needs to remember this today. We must stop relying on human planning, ideas, and strategies. Instead, we must come back to living and working in ways that grow from prayer, discernment, and faithfulness to Jesus' strategy: spiritual multiplication through relationships.

Rebekah – Prayer Can Conquer What Seems Impossible

Later in Genesis, Isaac prays that his wife will conceive a child, and his prayer is answered when Rebekah gets pregnant. This is simple. God grants the prayer of Isaac. What, in your view, does God want to accomplish through your work or your parish? God wants us to achieve great things for his sake. That means the Church must get up and get past our comfort zones. The start will come when we abandon ourselves to God's will through genuine faithful daily prayer.

Is deep prayer taking place within your family, parish, or diocese? Is it regular, personal, and intimate? I have witnessed this kind of prayer in Catholic groups and families, but it is not common enough. I think too many Church leaders have spiritual lives that are stunted, and they do not have deep spiritual relationships with anyone. With no good example in our midst, how can we know how to pray and discern as a people of God together? As a result, our groups and families fall victim to our own spiritual barrenness. We have to break the pattern and start praying individually and corporately—deeply and regularly—to be true people of prayer.

Rachel – Barrenness Comes from Loving God Less Than Anything Else

In Genesis 29–30, we see the story of Rachel and her sister Leah. Both are Jacob's wives. Leah has many sons; Rachel is barren. Rachel feels envy and begins to blame others, compete, and quarrel with her sister. She becomes angry with God. Finally, when God decides to do so and only when Rachel's heart is ready and grateful, he blesses Rachel with fertility. She rejoices in her children.

We often let our own wants and our pride get in God's way. We block his will. God wants us to be fruitful in having spiritual offspring and making disciples. But if we fail to love him above all others, our lack of love can lead to a barren spirituality. We have to repent and love God first in all things: time, money, sexuality, politics—everything. We must submit everything to God, including our goals for our parishes and apostolates.

God longs for us to be fruitful spiritually. To quote Pope Francis, when evangelization is "faithful to the Lord's gift, it also bears fruit. An evangelizing community is always concerned with fruit, because the Lord wants her to be fruitful."[28]

"By this my Father is glorified, that you bear much fruit, and so prove to be my disciples" (John 15:8).

JESUS MADE MULTIPLE

appearances to his followers after he rose from the grave. One of these is when he appeared to two disciples traveling to Emmaus. As they were walking along, Jesus came up next to them and asked what they were talking about. They told him they were discussing Jesus' death (not knowing it was Jesus they were talking to). They then expressed their disappointment because they were hoping he was the Messiah. Jesus opened the Scriptures to them and taught them that he had to suffer, die, and rise again. Then, when they reached their destination, he broke bread with them, their eyes were opened, and they recognized him.

We need our eyes opened. Jesus, we need you to draw alongside us as we attempt to grow as your disciples. Teach us. Guide us. Give us your life. Help us to be missionary disciples who see you when we break Bread in the Eucharist. Help us to have our hearts burn when we read your Scriptures. Teach us to be great evangelists so your name is glorified and more people go to heaven. This is what we desire.

QUESTIONS FOR CONSIDERATION

✳ *What are some top takeaways from this book?*

✳ *What are your current weaknesses and strengths as an evangelist?*

✳ *What goals do you have now that you did not have before starting this book?*

✳ *Who do you need to share these things with?*

APPENDIX 1

RESOURCES

Catechesis in Our Times (*Catechesi Tradendae*). John Paul II, apostolic exhortation, 1979.

Decree on the Apostolate of Lay People (*Apostolicam Actuositatem*). Vatican II.

Decree on the Church's Missionary Activity (*Ad Gentes*). Vatican II.

Dogmatic Constitution on the Church (*Lumen Gentium*). Vatican II.

Evangelization in the Modern World (*Evangelii Nuntiandi*). Paul VI, apostolic exhortation, 1975.

The Joy of the Gospel (*Evangelii Gaudium*). Francis, apostolic exhortation, 2013.

Disciples Called to Witness: The New Evangelization. Washington, DC: United States Conference of Catholic Bishops, 2012.

General Directory for Catechesis. Washington, DC: United States Conference of Catholic Bishops, 1998.

Everett Fritz. *The Art of Forming Young Disciples: Why Youth Ministries Aren't Working and What to Do About It.* Sophia Institute Press, 2018.

Fr. James Mallon. *Divine Renovation: Bringing Your Parish from Maintenance to Mission.* Twenty-Third Publications, 2014.

Curtis Martin. *Making Missionary Disciples: How to Live the Method Modeled by the Master.* FOCUS, 2018.

Sherry A. Weddell, editor. *Becoming a Parish of Intentional Disciples.* Our Sunday Visitor, 2015.

Sherry A. Weddell. *Forming Intentional Disciples: The Path to Knowing and Following Jesus.* Our Sunday Visitor, 2012.

André Regnier. *Clear & Simple: How to Have Conversations that Lead to Conversion.* Catholic Christian Outreach, 2018.

Deacon Keith Strohm. *Jesus: The Story You Thought You Knew.* Our Sunday Visitor, 2017.

Michael White and Tom Corcoran. *Rebuilt: Awakening the Faithful, Reaching the Lost, and Making Church Matter.* Ave Maria Press, 2012.

APPENDIX 2

WHAT THE BIBLE AND THE CHURCH SAY ABOUT THE *KERYGMA*

Here are some quotes about the *kerygma* from the Bible and Church documents:

- A description of the *kerygma*: "The initial ardent proclamation by which a person is one day overwhelmed and brought to the decision to entrust himself to Jesus Christ by faith" (John Paul II, *Catechesi Tradendae*, 25).

- "In the complex reality of mission, initial proclamation has a central and irreplaceable role, since it introduces man 'into the mystery of the love of God, who invites him to enter into a personal relationship with himself in Christ' and opens the way to conversion" (John Paul II, *Redemptoris Missio*, 44).

- "Woe to me if I do not preach the gospel" (1 Corinthians 9:16).

- "For what we preach is not ourselves, but Jesus Christ as Lord" (2 Corinthians 4:5).

- "I am eager to preach the gospel to you also who are in Rome. For I am not ashamed of the gospel: it is the power of God for salvation to every one who has faith" (Romans 1:15-16).

- "Even the finest witness will prove ineffective in the long run if it is not explained, justified—what Peter called always having 'your answer ready for people who ask you the reason for the hope that you all have'—and made explicit by a clear and unequivocal proclamation of the Lord Jesus. The Good News proclaimed by the witness of life sooner or later has to be proclaimed by the word of life. There is no true evangelization if the name, the teaching, the life, the promises, the kingdom and the mystery of Jesus of Nazareth, the Son of God are not proclaimed" (Paul VI, *Evangelii Nuntiandi*, 22).

- "An apostolate of this kind does not consist only in the witness of one's way of life; a true apostle looks for opportunities to announce Christ by words addressed either to non-believers with a view to leading them to faith, or to the faithful with a view to instructing, strengthening, and encouraging them to a more fervent life. 'For the charity of Christ impels us' (2 Cor. 5:14)" (*Apostolicam Actuositatem*, 6).

- "The preaching of the early Church was centered on the proclamation of Jesus Christ, with whom the kingdom was identified. Now, as then, there is a need to unite *the proclamation of the kingdom of God* (the content of Jesus' own "kerygma") and *the proclamation of the Christ-event* (the "kerygma" of the apostles). The two proclamations are complementary; each throws light on the other" (John Paul II, *Redemptoris Missio*, 16).

- "In catechesis too, we have rediscovered the fundamental role of the first announcement or kerygma, which needs to be the centre of all evangelizing activity and all efforts at Church renewal. ... [I]t is the principal proclamation, the one which we must hear again and again in different ways, the one which we must announce one way or another throughout the process of catechesis, at every level and moment" (Francis, *Evangelii Gaudium*, 164).

- "We must not think that in catechesis the kerygma gives way to a supposedly more 'solid' formation. Nothing is more solid, profound, secure, meaningful and wisdom-filled than that initial proclamation. All Christian formation consists of entering more deeply into the kerygma" (Francis, *Evangelii Gaudium*, 165).

NOTES

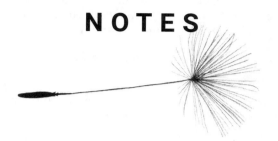

1. Paul VI, *Evangelii Nuntiandi* (December 8, 1975), 14.

2. Pew Research Center, *America's Changing Religious Landscape*, May 12, 2015, pewforum.org/.

3. *Gaudium et Spes* (December 7, 1965), 22, vatican.va/.

4. John Paul II, *Catechesi Tradendae* (October 16, 1979), 20, vatican.va/.

5. "Spiritual Multiplication," Cru, accessed August 20, 2019, cru.org/. See also *Focus*, "Teaching a Disciple to Share Spiritual Multiplication," 2017, focusoncampus.org/ and Brian McAdam, "Making Disciples of All Nations Through Spiritual Multiplication: Part 1 of 2," *Focus*, April 30, 2012, focusoncampus.org/.

6. *Focus*, "Teaching a Disciple to Share Spiritual Multiplication."

7. "Spiritual Multiplication," Cru. See also *Focus*, "Teaching a Disciple to Share Spiritual Multiplication" and Brian McAdam, "Making Disciples of All Nations Through Spiritual Multiplication: Part 1 of 2."

8. Sherry A. Weddell, *Forming Intentional Disciples: The Path to Knowing and Following Jesus* (Huntington, IN: Our Sunday Visitor, 2017), 127-130. In this chapter, I am summarizing chapters 5–8 of *Forming Intentional Disciples*.

9. Pew Research Center, "Chapter 1: Religious Beliefs and Practices," *U.S. Religious Landscape Survey: Religious Beliefs and Practices*, June 1, 2008, pewforum.org/.

10. Francis, homily, St. Francis Square, Assisi (October 4, 2013), vatican.va/.

11. Benedict XVI, "Message of His Holiness Pope Benedict XVI for the Twenty-Sixth World Youth Day (2011)" (August 6, 2010), vatican.va/.

12. *Ad Gentes* (December 7, 1965), 13, vatican.va/.

13. Thomas à Kempis, "The Intimate Friendship of Jesus," in *The Imitation of Christ*, accessed August 1, 2019, catholicarchive.org/.

14. John Paul II, *Catechesi Tradendae*, 19.

15. Ibid., 20.

16. Ibid., 19.

17. Francis, *Evangelii Gaudium* (November 24, 2013), 3, vatican.va/.

18. *General Directory for Catechesis* (Washington, DC: United States Conference of Catholic Bishops, 1998), 61.

19. "'Great Story' of Jesus in 9 'Acts' (Sherry Weddell)," in Marcel LeJeune, "The Content of the Kerygma – Good News for the World!" *Catholic Missionary Disciples*, accessed October 22, 2019, catholicmissionarydisciples.com/.

20. See Companions of the Cross, "The Kerygma – School of Evangelization (Talk 2) – Handout," accessed August 28, 2019, companionscross.org/.

21. Pope Paul VI, *Address to the Members of the Consilium de Laicis* (2 October 1974): AAS 66 (1974), p. 568, quoted in Paul VI, *Evangelii Nuntiandi*, 41.

22. Gregory DiPippo, ed., "A History of the 40 Hours Devotion, by Henri de Villiers," *New Liturgical Movement* (blog), March 7, 2018, newliturgicalmovement.org/.

23. Joe Heschmeyer, "The Evangelical and Pastoral Heart of St. Francis de Sales," *Word on Fire Blog*, January 24, 2018, wordonfire.org/. See also "St. Francis de Sales," Catholic Online, accessed August 27, 2019, catholic.org/.

24. Benedict XVI, "Message of the Holy Father Benedict XVI to the Young People of the World on the Occasion of the XXIII World Youth Day, 2008" (July 20, 2007), 4, vatican.va/.

25. Francis, *Evangelii Gaudium*, 259.

26. C. S. Lewis, *The Four Loves* (1960; repr. New York: Harcourt Brace & Company, 1988), 121, books.google.com/.

27. Committee on Evangelization and Catechesis, *Disciples Called to Witness: The New Evangelization* (Washington, DC: United States Conference of Catholic Bishops, 2012).

28. Francis, *Evangelii Gaudium*, 24.